The Deerholme Mushroom Cookbook

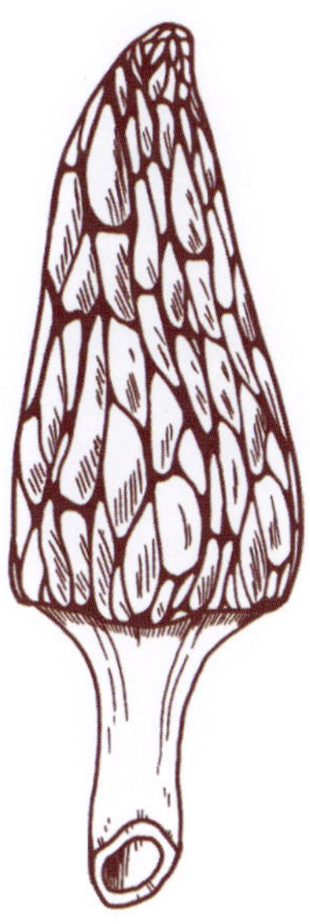

THE DEERHOLME

MUSHROOM COOKBOOK

FROM FORAGING TO FEASTING | REVISED AND UPDATED

Bill Jones

TOUCHWOOD

TouchWood Editions
touchwoodeditions.com

Editor: Holland Gidney
Proofreader: Cailey Cavallin
Cover and interior design: Sara Loos
Photos by Bill Jones unless annotated
Mushroom illustrations on pages i, 11, 45, 63, 89, 173, and 221 by Sydney Barnes.

CATALOGUING DATA AVAILABLE FROM LIBRARY AND ARCHIVES CANADA
ISBN 9781771514392 (softcover)
ISBN 9781771514408 (electronic)

TouchWood Editions acknowledges that the land on which we live and work is within the traditional territories of the Lkwungen (Esquimalt and Songhees), Malahat, Pacheedaht, Scia'new, T'Sou-ke andW̱SÁNEĆ (Pauquachin, Tsartlip, Tsawout, Tseycum) peoples.

We acknowledge the financial support of the Government of Canada through the Canada Book Fund and of the Province of British Columbia through the Book Publishing Tax Credit.

Canada   BRITISH COLUMBIA

This book was produced using FSC®-certified, acid-free papers, processed chlorine free, and printed with soya-based inks.

PRINTED IN CHINA

28 27 26 25 24 1 2 3 4 5

Dedicated to the memory of James Barber (1923–2007)
"These mushrooms are marvellous."

CONTENTS

OLIVER WITH PORCINI

INTRODUCTION

Most of our lives are spent wrapped in civilization. We are nestled in our cars, houses, offices, and landscapes. Stepping outside of this comfortable zone, we find the wildness lurking at the edges of our world. It is here that the mushrooms live, waiting to feed us, kill us, heal us, or alter our perception of reality. *But which ones do what?* That is a really good question. Such a question started me on my journey into the world of fungi. Little did I know it would be a path of fascination, delight, and wonder that has kept me learning for more than twenty years. Mushrooms, or more correctly *mycelia*, wrap the planet like an intricate web. They are critical to plant life and important to the rest of us passengers on this planet. Mushrooms are harvested by ants, nibbled by deer and rabbits, and hunted for the table. Scientists study them to find new drugs, feed livestock, and heal damaged environments. Mushrooms may one day be eating our plastics, curing our cancers, and helping to reduce the damage we have rained on Mother Nature.

Mushrooms have also fuelled my dreams. Walking through a quiet forest, I've smelled the aroma of pine mushrooms and uncovered their secrets from underneath a mossy blanket. It's a happy dream, one that triggers fond memories each time it occurs in real life. Foraging in the wild reaches back to some primordial part of me that would have been happy roasting chunks of meat over an open campfire. It is hard to describe the pure pleasure you get from finding a prime mushroom like the porcini, pine mushroom, or morel. The porcini is a plump, golden object of beauty. Like a painting by Raphael, it celebrates the curves and sensuality of nature. But the porcini can also be a source of vast disappointment. Finding a large, mature specimen often means finding a mushroom chock full of fungus gnat maggots, tiny worms spoiling the sweet flesh. Yes, the porcini is the heartbreak mushroom—but then again so are the pine, the lobster mushroom, and many others.

My first mushroom awakening occurred through my culinary pursuits. In France, I was introduced to the *cèpe* (as the French call the porcini). At first glance, the appearance is alluring: a

CLOCKWISE FROM TOP: CHANTERELLES ON MOSS, GLASS MUSHROOM, ARTISAN CARVING.

velvety, brown cap resting on a swollen base. At first bite, it's a revelation of flavour: meaty and earthy, with notes of caramel and spice. I imagine my eyebrows arched in surprise as I chewed that first mouthful. My perception of mushrooms as white buttons in the grocery store changed forever on that day. It was love at first bite.

As I began to research and uncover the mystery of mushrooms, it became apparent this was a big topic, a really big topic. Now, some twenty years later, I have explored many trails and paths, read books, talked to experts, and still have mountains more to uncover. There have been many revelatory moments: Learning to read the trees and plant life for clues to the presence of mushrooms. Learning which mushrooms to avoid and which will boost my health. I have also discovered that one of my favourite varieties is still the humble button mushroom.

Foraging for mushrooms is a seasonal pursuit. Spring brings us out of our winter slumbers with sweet blossoms and the promise of morels. Late summer gifts us with field mushrooms and the first chanterelles. But fall is by far my favourite time of the year. Crisp clear nights, autumn rains rinsing the landscape, and the welcome explosion of mushrooms. When September hits, we head off into the forest to track the progress of our best mushroom patches. Along the way, we sample the last of the summer blackberries and the newly ripening salal berries. Often the bears have the same idea and we see traces of their presence around the berry patches (scat) and in holes dug in stumps and logs (where they have been looking for grubs and ants). Fortunately they don't seem too fussed about mushrooms. And finally in winter, while we rest up before beginning the cycle anew, nature gives us truffles to console us and stockpiles of dried and preserved mushrooms to keep us amused.

I am fortunate to live in the Cowichan Valley on Vancouver Island, one of the most wondrous areas on earth for mushrooms. Giant chanterelles, plump boletes, majestic cauliflower mushrooms, and firm, dense pine mushrooms are hidden in the landscape. I forage in the mature forests of the region and look for patches of healthy moss, often on the slopes and plateaus of the valley. The mushrooms I have described in this book occur in some form all over the planet, but the temperate bands between the equator and both poles yield the conditions for producing the best edible mushrooms.

Cultivated mushrooms have copied the work of nature and free us from a dependence on seasonality and location. This is why the shiitake mushrooms of Asia are now a locally grown product found in our markets. Mushroom growers have made the culinary and health-promoting properties of fungi available year-round.

In my classes, food demos, and cooking, I always try to use a variety of wild and cultivated mushrooms. They are tasty and good for you in many ways. The recipes in this book use global cooking techniques found in many cultures, inspired by Italian risotto, Chinese dim sum, Spanish tapas, and backyard grilling over a fire. Using your own creativity to alter the dishes is encouraged. These recipes work with many types of mushrooms. There is a great saying in stone masonry: "the best stones to build with are the ones you have to carry the shortest distance." It is much the same with mushrooms: the best mushrooms to cook with are the ones you have available. The results will be different, but all are interesting and enjoyable on some level. Some mushrooms just taste better than others. That's why the porcini, morels, and truffles are the rock stars of the fungi world.

What is important is to focus on fresh, locally grown products. Here on Vancouver Island, we are blessed with the ingredient bounty of the Pacific Northwest. This book is a celebration of seasonal and local foods. In that spirit, seek out the best local food products you can find, support small farmers, or grow your own produce when possible. The planet and your immune system will thank you.

But what's the catch? Foraging for mushrooms requires education, experience, and, above all, respect. It may not be for the faint of heart, but it may be the key to strengthening your heart. In life, there are always choices. This book tries to impart a little of the knowledge needed to make these choices. I have discovered these secrets reading books, hanging out with mycologists, and attending workshops. However, mainly I have learned by walking along forest trails, and through observing and asking the right questions before I ultimately eat any new mushroom. The cooking part was arrived at through a similar process: eating in restaurants, working in professional kitchens, and sitting around the campfire roasting chunks of meat. Now I get to pass that knowledge on to you.

Never eat a mushroom when you are not 100 percent sure of its identity. Taste a little bit of any identified mushroom the first time you eat it. Many people have allergies or reactions to common fungi, including the ones found in the supermarket. In the wild, remember that mushrooms can kill you; that fact should always have your full attention.

That said, always try to have fun when foraging. Start with the low-hanging fruit, like chanterelles, and work your way up to the harder species. Join a mycological society or find a mentor to guide your education. Use this book as a launching pad to propel your journey into the world of mushrooms.

I am proud and humbled to live, work, and play on the ancestral and unceded territories of the Quw'utsun, Malahat, Halalt, Ts'uubaa-asatx, Penelakut, Stz'uminus, Lyackson, Pauquachin, Ditidaht, and Pacheedaht Peoples.

Bill Jones
Cowichan Valley
Vancouver Island, BC

A few of my favourite mushroom-foraging sayings:

"There are old mushroom foragers and bold mushroom foragers—there are no old bold mushroom foragers." —Anon.

"Any mushroom is edible—once." —Anon.

"I confess that nothing frightens me more than the appearance of mushrooms on the table, especially in a small provincial town." —Alexander Dumas (1802-1870)

And then there is . . .
"One side will make you taller and one side will make you shorter," said the caterpillar.
"What side of what?" asked Alice.
"The mushroom, of course," replied the caterpillar.
—Lewis Carroll, *Alice's Adventures in Wonderland* (1865)

Deerholme Farm (a little history)

Deerholme is more than a farm in the Cowichan Valley of Vancouver Island. It is the fulfillment of a dream that germinated while toiling in the kitchens of restaurants and strolling farmers' markets in many parts of the world. My wife Lynn and I had long talked about having our own place, somewhere to grow an edible landscape and forage from the local fields, forests, and oceans. We also wanted to be part of a community, working with like-minded individuals and helping those around us who were just starting out—giving back to the community and those less fortunate than ourselves.

Looking back, these concepts were not very revolutionary—we simply sought to create an environment where we were able to control the quality and source of our food. Along the way we were inspired by the people who had blazed the trail before us. Meeting Michael Stadtländer from Eigensinn Farm was a watershed moment. He had managed to create a farm restaurant that was open only on weekends and generated a world-wide reputation for excellence in the process. On the island, working with Sinclair and Fredrica Philip (Sooke Harbour House), Mara Jernigan (Fairburn Farm) and Michael Ableman (Foxglove Farm) and artisan producers like Hillary and Patty Abbott (Hillary's Cheese) was inspirational in making our community vibrant and exciting to be a part of.

Over the course of the years, we renovated our old farmhouse, turning it into a cozy venue for local food dinners, cooking classes, and wild food workshops. It is our realization of the foodie dream. We have planted many types of gardens on our property. Herbs, salad greens, vegetables, orchards, and fruit cages are scattered about the landscape. We harvest these gifts from the garden and supplement them with the wild foods growing around the trails and fields of the valley. The ocean is also a bountiful supermarket of edible wonders. We take inspiration from the local First Nations and have learned to love the land as they do. Most of our other products come from people we know on a first-name basis. Many are friends who have share our good times, broken bread at our tables, or helped out in times of need, like good neighbours do.

Looking back on our journey, we have achieved most of what we set out to do—we have created an edible Eden, set apart from the world of mass production and churning food factories. We celebrate the labours of our hands, the skills of our community, and the flavours that only good, healthy food can produce.

FUNDAMENTALS

What Are Mushrooms?

Mushrooms are members of the Fungi kingdom and are distinct from other classifications of plants and animals. For the purposes of the mushroom enthusiast, mushrooms are the fruiting body of a larger organism composed of a complex network of fibres called mycelia. A great analogy is to think of mushrooms as the fruit of mycelia, much like apples are the fruit of an apple tree.

Among the most interesting mushrooms to foragers are the mycorrhizal fungi that grow in symbiotic (beneficial to both) relationship with trees and plants. These mushrooms work closely with the plants to extend the reach of their roots. In doing so, the mushrooms bring back nutrients and moisture to the plant in exchange for sugars produced through photosynthesis. Mushrooms lack chlorophyll and thus cannot produce these sugars themselves. This is an important concept for the forager because certain trees will always associate with good edible mushrooms. For example, the Douglas fir is a host tree for a wide range of edible mushrooms, including the famous chanterelle. The earliest fossilized record of mycorrhizal fungi goes back some 400 million years so the ecology of the entire planet is firmly dependent on our fungi friends.

Furthermore, mycelium webs can overlap and many types of mushrooms can be present in the same small space of forest. Edible mushrooms live happily next to poisonous mushrooms.

Mushrooms tend to require certain conditions to fruit in abundance. Many mushrooms fruit in the fall, after the dry days of summer have given way to cool rains. In viewing the harvest cycle over many years, I have seen an amazingly diverse group of mushrooms fruit in the same area, depending on the unique conditions each year brings. In general, rain followed by gentle warm sunshine is the best scenario for producing lots of good edible mushrooms. Under such conditions, the more it rains, the more mushrooms are produced. This cycle of growth continues through the fall as temperatures dip and days become shorter. Here in the Pacific Northwest, we can keep harvesting until late November or December, pickling a bumper crop of mushrooms. The harvest only stops when we get consecutive days of freezing temperatures. This is the killing frost that both gardeners and fungi lovers dislike.

Saprophytic mushrooms are a second important class of fungi. These are Mother Nature's recyclers: they feed on dead and decaying materials. They are doubly important because this process can easily be repeated in a commercial growing operation, which is one way to produce button mushrooms (*Agaricus* sp.), shiitakes, oysters, enoki, and many others.

Lovely saprophytic mushrooms also occur in the forest, and one of the tastiest is the cauliflower fungus—a beautiful and delicious find for the forager. Locally the cauliflower is found on the giant stumps of Douglas fir trees that were cut down many years ago. Saprophytes also appear in sawdust piles, compost heaps, bales of straw, and wood chips. Mushroom spawn is introduced by spores into these dead materials and the mycelium feeds, grows, and fruits on top.

Third on the fungi hit list is the ascomycetes group, which famously includes the morel and truffle families. Morels like to start fruiting in the spring after the retreat of winter snows (or following the rainy season in milder climates). Certain morels also like to pop up a season or two after a forest fire; they seem to like the lack of competition (from plants, other mycelia, etc.) that a forest fire creates. In general, ascomycetes are a little unusual because they reproduce using spores found in tiny sacs inside the organism, while most mushrooms (with some exceptions, like puffballs) reproduce using spores found in the gills and tubes underneath their caps.

Parasitic mushrooms are the fourth major classification. Here we find mushrooms that also interact with a host to extract nutrients, but the relationship often does not end well for the host. The lobster mushroom is one of the best examples of this process. The host mushroom is attacked by the parasitic fungus, which converts it into a lobster mushroom. Other mushrooms feed on trees (including the destructive honey mushroom *Armillaria* sp.) and even caterpillars (*Cordyceps* sp.). Cordyceps are renowned for their medicinal properties and are one of the most powerful tools in traditional Chinese medicine. They are becoming more important to conventional medicine too as we discover and test the benefits of medicinal mushrooms.

There are other oddball classifications of fungi but these four main categories provide us with the most joy when eating, foraging, and cultivating mushrooms. Even so, the details are immense and can become a little convoluted—and there are many exceptions to what I have laid out here, as scientists uncover more and more each day about this fascinating world.

What Do We Call You, Dear Fungi?

When looking into the world of fungi, you always end up with the old dilemma of scientific versus common names. Mushrooms occur all over the world, and in each region people have local names for particular mushrooms. Consider the porcini, which is an Italian name that translates to "little piglet." I love this name and use it frequently. But travel to France and the name changes to cèpe, which translates to "tree trunk." Journey on to Germany and you will find the same mushroom called *Steinpilz*, which means, "stone mushroom"—and on and on.

Scientists do not believe in such frivolous naming games; they go back to Latin (because everyone knows Latin, right?) to describe each mushroom by a genus (family name) and a species (a more descriptive identifier). Thus, the porcini becomes *Boletus edulis*. By the way, *edulis* is Latin for "edible," which is always a good sign. With only one correct scientific name (*B. edulis*) and many possible common names, things hummed along fantastically for many years until we started studying fungi in greater detail and brought techniques like DNA analysis into the picture.

Nowadays, scientific names are continually being revised and updated. North American mushrooms may be identical to European mushrooms, or they may be new species altogether, such as the newly named pacific golden chanterelle. For years, what we called *Cantharellus cibarius* mycologists now call *Cantharellus formosus*. It's like a giant soap opera that only excites the inner mushroom nerd in some of us. I tend to call mushrooms by my favourite common name and include its scientific name as a tribute to scientific righteousness.

SOURCING MUSHROOMS

Foraging For Mushrooms

Obviously the best opportunity to get fresh mushrooms is to forage for them yourself. The drawback is the danger of misidentifying mushrooms with dangerous consequences. Many of the shopping tips that follow also apply to mushrooms in the field. You should be looking for prime specimens, free of imperfections, insects, and mould. Transport your mushrooms with care; some species, such as the parasol mushroom, are delicate and will easily break down if handled roughly. Please see the foraging section (p. 11) for more specific details.

Shopping For Mushrooms

Not all of us have the opportunity or the ability to forage for mushrooms. Luckily there is growing consumer demand for these products and the grocery industry is starting to carry a wider array of exotic types of mushrooms. You still have to be cautious when buying mushrooms in stores, since store staff are usually not well versed in keeping mushrooms fresh over a longer period of time. Stores rely on a quick turnover to keep the product fresh. You often see mushrooms for sale that are far past the point of ultimate freshness. Mushrooms are mainly water, and over time they dry out, particularly when on display in the vegetable section of a market. Each mushroom type can require a different method of storage and grocers are simply not trained in these methods. Adding water to some mushroom types may, in fact, speed their decay. Please see the shopping section (p. 45) for more information.

Growing Your Own

Harvesting your own mushroom crop is an option that has become much more mainstream over the last few years. The setup can be as simple as a plastic bag filled with wood chips inoculated with mushroom spawn. You place the bundle away from direct sun in a location indoors or outdoors where you can mist the mushrooms with water as they grow. If you have space outside, you can set up a shiitake log or two to produce mushrooms over a much longer period of time. The drawbacks of both methods are mainly letting the mushroom medium dry out, which kills the organism, and the occasional infestation of fungus gnats attracted by the aromatic mushrooms. Please see the growing section (p. 63) for more information.

Legnoart

FORAGING FOR MUSHROOMS

New foragers tend to stress out over the potential of eating a poisonous mushroom. Truth be told, you are far more likely to fall prey to the environment around you. The wilderness is sometimes an inhospitable place. Mossy slopes, downed trees, sinkholes, thorns, and thick brush all lurk quietly, waiting to twist an ankle or break a bone. An act that would require a call to an ambulance or a visit to an emergency room in the city can turn into a life-threatening situation in the deep woods. As a result, you will benefit from some basic survival knowledge and an awareness of the potential dangers that await foragers.

PLANNING

The first rule of thumb is to never venture into the woods alone. Keep in mind that your iPhone might be the best thing since sliced bread in the city, but it often has a very limited range in the deep woods. Always tell someone where you are going and when you expect to return. Too much can go wrong in the woods: cellphone calls drop, batteries die, the weather changes rapidly. Foraging is always better with company too; make it an act of sharing and you will be safer and happier.

FORAGING GEAR

There are a few things I always bring with me on a forage. Here is my checklist:

- Cellphone
- Pocket knife of good quality, i.e., Swiss Army (I put mine on a cord or lanyard)
- Compass (take a reading of the position of your car from the forest edge)
- Backpack, small size
- Food: sandwich, fruit, chocolate, granola bar, etc.
- Survival kit: matches, foil blanket, granola bar, bandages, safety pins, etc.
- Gloves (and a hat if it's cold out)
- Raincoat (I prefer Gore-Tex, which is a breathable, water-repellant fabric)
- Optional: wristwatch, camera, GPS device

POTENTIAL HAZARDS

Getting Lost

While foraging, there is a tendency to do two dangerous things. One is to look at the ground as you walk. The second is to get carried away by the thrill of the forage. Particularly when you are finding lots of mushrooms, the thrill tends to make you forget important things like direction. The natural tendency for most people is to veer to the left or right when they are walking (even though they may think they are walking in a straight line). The best low-tech source of direction is often the sun, but it is not helpful when it is cloudy or raining. I like to keep an eye on stream direction and the general layout of hills as I hike. It is also useful to bring along a topographic map to orient yourself with major features in the area where you are foraging. A compass (or GPS device) is your best friend in the deep woods.

Natural Hazards

Deadfall, rotted stumps, and soft moss are all part of the hazards of foraging. Rotting stumps are particularly treacherous as they can allow your leg to suddenly sink deep into the moss, a potential threat to your bones and knee ligaments. Your best defence is a good pair of hiking boots. They provide good ankle support, which helps lessen the stress and sudden twisting of your legs if you do make a misstep. High winds are another dangerous hazard in the woods, causing tree branches to break off or trees to uproot and turning dead trees into dangerous projectiles. Check the weather forecast before leaving and avoid foraging in areas with high wind warnings. Leave the woods quickly if a sudden storm kicks up.

Wildlife

It is fairly common to see animals like bears while foraging for mushrooms in the woods. After all they do live there and you are the one invading their living room.

Happily, **bears** will often run away and leave you alone. They have poor eyesight, so they will hear and smell you before they see you. You should be concerned, though, if you see a freshly killed carcass or spot small bear cubs nearby. Slowly back away from bears and head off in the opposite direction. If you are placed in a bad position (i.e., being attacked), you can try using bear spray (hot pepper spray) or hitting the bear sharply in the nose or eyes repeatedly. This is easier said than done since a black bear can weigh up to 1,500 pounds (680 kg) and has very strong teeth and claws. Bears will often try to attack your head and neck, so the best advice is to curl up in a ball and wrap your hands around your neck. Actually, the very best advice is to avoid a confrontation altogether—it is far less painful.

Cougars are another local threat here in the Pacific Northwest. Although naturally shy, cougars are attracted to dogs and small children. They hunt

I have probably met more than 50 bears in my travels but the only real incident was when I had left bacon in my backpack and one night a bear decided to eat my backpack to get at this treat. Fortunately, the only casualty was my pack (and my bacon), which was hanging in a tree near my tent.

around dusk, so it is never a good idea to be foraging at this time of day. Cougar attacks are more common if the cougar's natural food sources (deer, rabbits, etc.) are scarce or the animal is in distress and desperate. If you see a cougar, you should be very concerned. Yell and try to make yourself look big by raising your arms.

Ticks are a common pest in the boreal forest. Be sure to remove any ticks as soon as possible: they may be only a mild irritant, but they do occasionally harbour harmful bacteria. In particular, Lyme disease is a serious infection with debilitating side effects. The classic symptoms are a circular, expanding rash around the bite, followed by severe and persistent flu-like systems (sometimes lasting months). The best protection against ticks is covering your skin with clothing, tucking your pants into your socks, and wearing a hat. While they are somewhat rare in the Pacific Northwest, ticks can have serious consequences.

Poisonous Mushrooms

I remember buying a vintage cookbook called *Maori Cooking of New Zealand*. Imagine my delight when I discovered it contained a chapter on mushrooms. The chapter heading was a gem. In the Maori language, *mushroom* translates to "food that can attack." Someone must have learned the hard way.

That said, the vast majority of mushrooms are fairly tame. There are reputed to be as many as 7,000 species of fungi in the Pacific Northwest, and, of that number, fewer than 50 species are choice edibles. Of the rest, there is a tiny handful that can kill, with a much larger number (hundreds) that can cause illness, physical discomfort, or permanent damage. So the good news is that it's not easy to kill yourself but it's entirely possible!

COMMON MORELS

One of my favourite stories concerns the beautiful and deadly *Amanita verna*. It is a mushroom that is majestic, firm, and pure white. It is also a deadly mushroom known as the destroying angel. Someone once described it as "the best mushroom I've ever eaten, sweet and delicious" mere days before he died of complete organ failure. These deadly mushrooms contain amatoxins, which interfere with kidney and liver function. The organs shut down and the results are not pleasant (coma, death), unless an organ transplant is performed.

The general rule I follow is to ignore most of the mushrooms that are difficult to identify and stick with learning the ones you will have the highest chance of positively identifying. I outline these varieties on the pages that follow. (Many guides include other types of edible mushrooms that are rewarding if you put in the homework to understand and appreciate the tiny details.) My caution list includes the fairy ring mushrooms (*Marasmius oreades*), blewits (*Lepista nuda*), and edible amanitas like Caesar's mushroom (*Amanita caesarea*). They are all delicious mushrooms but they are also easily confused with seriously poisonous mushrooms. Remember, "a little knowledge is dangerous."

I highly recommend you sign up for a mushroom foraging workshop or join your local mycological society (see Resources, p. 267). Going out with experts is a great way to get introduced to the foraging world.

RECOMMENDED VARIETIES

Morels

The morel is an unmistakable mushroom, with a sponge-like head and a pale, hollow body. Morels are delicious fresh or dried and are one of the top culinary mushrooms. They are difficult to forage as they tend to blend in with the surrounding landscape. Morels grow in older growth forests, abandoned orchards, and gardens, and along roads and on sandy stream banks. The old saying "morels grow anywhere but not everywhere" is a true description of the fickle nature of the fungi. Although generally associated with spring, morels can appear in all the

COUNTERLOCKWISE FROM TOP: MILLA WHITEHEAD WITH LARGE MORELS (PHOTO BY ERIC WHITEHEAD), PORCINI (PHOTO BY ERIC WHITEHEAD), PINE MUSHROOM

seasons. It also appears that the mycelia of some morel species may be short-lived. This may add to the difficulty we have tracking morels in the same locations from year to year. Other mushroom types are more dependable and tend to fruit in much the same location.

In an average spring, morels appear soon after the crocus flowers bloom. In other areas, they fruit when the trillium flowers arrive. Thousands of morels will often sprout the year following a forest fire. Morels seem to like disturbances and often sprout from road cuts, excavations, and fallen trees. You can also buy morel spawn to inoculate your gardens and bark mulch, but it should be noted these kits have a low rate of success.

Morels should always be eaten cooked. Raw mushrooms can cause allergic reactions in some people. As well, a significant number of people exhibit dizziness and mild tremors when they combine morels and alcohol.

Black Morel (*Morchella brunnea* or *Morchella frustrata*) One of the first morels to appear in the spring. Commonly distributed all over the planet, the black morel occurs in Europe, Asia, and North and South America. Scientist think there are up to twelve varieties of black morels in North America. The black varieties are particularly difficult to see in the forest. The head looks almost identical to a fallen pinecone. The mushroom occurs early in the spring and may be present well into summer. The black morel can also occur in high alpine meadows, fruiting much later than morels at a lower altitude. Look for black morels under conifers, poplars, and shrub undergrowth. They seem to particularly like to fruit under aspen and pine trees but are found in a wide range of habitat. *M. frustrata* is a particularly strange mushroom as it appears creamy white or yellowish when younger, taking on a grey tone when mature.

Common Morel, or Yellow Morel (*Morchella snyderi* or *Morchella importuna*) After the blacks have begun to slow their fruiting, the common morel steps up to the plate. It can fruit in huge numbers if the conditions are right and is often found at lower elevations than other morels. The common morel prefers the late spring and needs a long, warm spell of weather following a cold winter. One of the most commonly hunted mushrooms, they seem to be partial to apple and cherry orchards, as well as aspen forests, but also appear in a wide variety of habitats. *M. importuna* is sometimes called the landscape morel. It often pops up in new bark mulch placed in gardens. It will usually fruit for the first year, then ultimately fade away.

Burnsite Morel, Black Foot Morel, or Fuzzy Foot Morel (*Morchella tomentosa, Morchella sextelata, Morchella septimelata,* or *Morchella captata*) A variation of the black morel, the burnsite morel occurs up to two years following a forest fire, usually reproducing in prolific amounts. It is thought that these morels are the first to return after a fire to take advantage of the lack of competition from other mushrooms. The morels feed on the burnt plant materials on the forest floor and help recycle the nutrients. These morels will have a distinct smoky flavour, particularly when dried.

Western White Morel (*Morchella rufobrunnea*) A recent addition to the scientific catalogue that was, up until 1998, referred to as *Morchella deliciosa* by many authors. The *deliciosa* is confined to the eastern portion of North America and to Europe. It is also related to the common morel but differs in subtle anatomical details. The white morel is one of the tastiest members of the morel family. The white morel seems to like steep slopes and plateaus. It also likes older growth forests of conifer trees.

Half-Free Morel (*Morchella populiphila*) Often found fruiting in sandy soil, along streams and lakes. Unlike the common morel, where the cap is completely attached to the stalk of the fungus, the half-free morel's sponge-like cap is only partially connected near the top of the stalk. It is a good edible but is more fragile and prone to collapsing and crushing after picking. Handle gently and you will be rewarded with a soft-textured mushroom with a delicate morel flavour.

Chanterelles

The fungi of the chanterelle family come in many strange and wonderful colours, from pale, creamy white to psychedelic shades of electric blue. Yellow chanterelles are abundant in the Pacific Northwest and the forests often provide bumper crops. On many occasions I have encountered several hundred chanterelles within a short hike. Readily available in public markets and specialty stores, chanterelles are continually gaining wider exposure. Dried chanterelles are a step down in quality from fresh ones, as the drying process renders the mushroom very tough, with a slightly bitter and peppery taste. However, frozen chanterelles are a good addition to soups and stews. Canned chanterelles are also occasionally available, generally imported from Europe.

The yellow chanterelle is probably the best mushroom with which to start your foraging career. It is fairly easy to identify, abundant, and doesn't look like it will kill you (always a bonus). The chanterelle occurs over most of the temperate zones of the planet. It is beloved in Europe, Asia, North America, South America, and South Africa. The chanterelle also happens to taste great, making it a good mushroom to get to know.

Chanterelle, Yellow Chanterelle, or Pacific Golden Chanterelle (*Cantharellus formosus*) Yellow chanterelles are many people's favourite wild mushroom. They have a beautiful, elegant form, are plentiful, and possess several unique characteristics. The bright yellow-orange colour also allows them to stick out from the forest floor.

The yellow chanterelle really likes locations with a deep, lush carpet of moss along with a fairly mature canopy of trees. I've had great success in older second-growth forests and mature (15- to 20-year-old) third-growth forests. Find one chanterelle and a careful search will usually turn up more hiding under the surrounding trees. In France, a smaller variety of chanterelle is known as the *girolle* (*Cantharellus cibarius*), which may also occur in eastern North America. Our Pacific variety is known for its huge size and paler underside. There is a second large northwest variety called *Cantharellus cascadensis*. It is very similar to the *C. formosus*, but with a slightly brighter yellow cap and a thin, wavy edge. Look in flat, forested areas at the base of hills and work your way up the slopes. They tend to fruit in clusters in coniferous, mossy forests. In some parts of the world, they are associated with beech and birch forests. Yellow chanterelles occur all over North America.

White Chanterelle (*Cantharellus subalbidus*) This delicious chanterelle is a cousin of the yellow chanterelle. Its colour is pale white to cream when fresh. After picking, the mushrooms often discolour around the edges and the

CLOCKWISE FROM TOP: PACIFIC GOLDEN CHANTERELLES, CLUSTERED BLUE CHANTERELLES, HEDGEHOG MUSHROOM

flesh appears to be slightly bruised, with darker shades of orange. The stem of the white chanterelle is often much thicker than that of the common yellow varieties. The flesh is tender and mild, and it is one of the best mushrooms for chowders and soups. The white chanterelle is often found in great numbers. However, the flesh can become saturated if there is too much moisture, and the mushrooms are sometimes attacked by fungus gnats and moulds near the end of the season. The white chanterelle does not like cold temperatures and will rot quickly if frozen. Look for white chanterelles at the edges of coniferous forests and in stands of salal and ferns.

Winter Chanterelle, Yellow Foot Chanterelle, or Funnel Chanterelle (*Craterellus tubaeformis*) A common late-season mushroom, particularly after heavy rains. It was formerly called *Cantharellus tubaeformis*. They are tasty sautéed and are often found in dried mushroom mixtures (particularly those from France). This delicate mushroom quickly loses its shape after picking and can degenerate into a soggy, larvae-infected mass if not stored properly. Wrap the mushrooms in plenty of paper towels, and refrigerate in a container that provides lots of side ventilation. Drying the mushroom actually helps to concentrate the flavour and results in a pleasing, firm texture. Locally we find the winter chanterelle among Douglas fir and hemlock trees.

Blue Chanterelle, Black Chanterelle, or Clustered Blue Chanterelle (*Polyozellus multiplex*) A delicious and unusual mushroom with a bluish-grey to black underside that often appears dusted with a pale white bloom. The blue chanterelle is excellent when sautéed in olive oil with minced garlic. This mushroom does tend to bleed a dark grey colour when cooked and will discolour white dishes like risotto and mashed potatoes. It grows in groups near mature hardwoods like oaks and poplars. In northern climates the mushroom is found in mature spruce and fir forests with banks of mature moss. The mushroom contains a compound called polyozellin that may potentially inhibit the growth of stomach cancers.

Black Chanterelle, Trumpet of Death, or Horn of Plenty (*Craterellus cornucopioides*) Looks like a delicate tube of black mushroom with a curled rim. They are excellent dried (some would say better). In France they are called the poor man's truffle, mainly for their appearance when chopped up and added to terrines and pâtés. They have a deep mushroom flavour that works best with stock-based sauces. They will turn a cream sauce an unappetizing shade of grey. The mushroom tends to associate with beech and oak trees. They also tend to like the fringes of the forest, where daylight can reach the forest floor. The trumpet is fairly rare in the Pacific Northwest but common in the middle of the continent down to Mexico. California is a particularly fertile habitat for the mushroom.

Pig's Ear, or Violet Chanterelle (*Gomphus clavatus*) An attractive mushroom with a purplish to violet tinge to the gills. It looks similar to a chanterelle but is clustered in groups and the flesh is far more fragile. We commonly find these mushrooms in older growth stands of trees, often in moist areas, such as near the edges of streams. In the Pacific Northwest, the forests are predominantly fir trees with a few spruce often present. The mushroom has a fine flavour and is excellent dried. Older specimens are often riddled with worms.

Boletes

The bolete family is a large group of mushrooms. Underneath the cap of the mushroom you will find a sponge-like texture instead of the gills that many fungi have. The most famous member is *Boletus edulis*, often called the porcini (or King Bolete), for its plump demeanour and superior flavour. The European boletes often have a deeper, sweeter flavour than many of our regional varieties. This might be due to our large local rainfall, which causes the mushroom to grow rapidly and often results in a soft, spongy texture. The better-tasting varieties often come from areas with relatively less rainfall. Mushrooms from high alpine areas also tend to have a better texture than the lowland varieties.

Boletes are among the safest mushrooms to forage. The sponge-like cap is very distinctive and no members of the family are deadly poisonous. A few boletes are bitter, but they can be avoided by following a few simple rules (see below).

Edible boletes are all very good when dried. Their pungent, earthy flavour is wonderful for making stocks, soups, and mushroom infusions. Check boletes carefully for the presence of small worms, which like to burrow in through the stem and eat the flesh. An infected mushroom

will appear soft and spongy—unappetizing for cooking or freezing. It still may have pieces that are suitable for drying. If the mushroom is completely riddled with worm trails, throw it out in the forest. If you are lucky, and have good karma, you may seed the woods with more porcini. Commercial bolete mixes often contain a mixture of many species; the more expensive ones contain only, or at least a high percentage of, *Boletus edulis*.

Porcini, King Bolete, Cèpe, Steinpilz, Penny Bun, etc. (*Boletus edulis*)—Characterized by a fat, light-brown top and a distinctive swollen base. There is some debate over the species name of our Pacific Northwest porcini—it may actually be a different species, but that has yet to be determined. When the mushroom is young, the undercap is whitish and firm. As the mushroom ages, the undercap becomes yellow to green and finally brown as it begins to break down. Also look for small pinholes on the sponge, which are signs that worms have penetrated the flesh.

It is by far the most prized mushroom in most of Europe and is known by several different local names. Porcini in the marketplace are often cut in half to display their inner flesh. This is done as quality control to check the mushroom for the presence of worms and also to ensure that the texture is firm and not soft. Soft-fleshed porcini are often bitter and can have a slimy texture. Firm, small porcini buttons freeze well. Cook them partially frozen for the best results. Look for porcini in two habitats: near the ocean in the undergrowth at the top of beaches and on forested slopes and in high alpine areas, particularly near lakes and streams. Top-quality mushrooms display a firm, creamy texture, free of rusty worm trails. At lower elevations you can often find a similar cousin called *Boletus fibrillosus*, which is distinguished by its deep-brown cap and somewhat slimmer base. It is also a good edible bolete but lacks the nutty richness of the porcini.

Other Edible Boletes: *Boletus* species, *Leccinum* species, and *Suillus* species—There are many boletes. Some are delectable and a few are kind of boring. Often it's the texture that puts people off, as they tend to have a slippery consistency when cooked. A few are considered poisonous, but they are quite rare. The boletes that stain blue (when pressed) seem to give people the most trouble.

COUNTERCLOCKWISE FROM TOP: SCABER BOLETES, BEAR'S PAW FUNGUS MUSHROOM, COMMON MORELS

One such bolete is called Satan's bolete (*Boletus satanas*), a fleshy mushroom that exhibits a deep-red, spongy mass under the cap and stains blue when pressed or cut. The mushroom is toxic when raw and has been reputed to cause great digestive stress. In general, boletes are a relatively safe group to forage.

Besides the ones already mentioned, here are a few other boletes to explore:

- Admirable Bolete—*Boletus mirabilis*
- Smith's Bolete—*Boletus smithii*
- Zeller's Bolete—*Boletus zelleri*
- Orange-Capped Bolete—*Leccinum aurantiacum*
- Scaly-Stemmed Bolete—*Leccinum scabrum*
- Slippery Jack—*Suillus luteus*
- Short-Stemmed Slippery Jack—*Suillus brevipes*
- Hollow-Stemmed Larch Bolete—*Suillus cavipes*
- Dotted-Stalk Slippery Jack—*Suillus granulatus*
- Lake's Bolete—*Suillus lakei*
- Olive-Capped Bolete—*Suillus subolivaceus*

Pine Mushrooms

The pine mushroom is a highly valued species and has been a member of the fungi elite in Asia for hundreds of years. In Japan, it is called the *matsutake* and is considered to have medicinal and aphrodisiac properties. The Pacific Northwest has been identified as a region with vast numbers of pine mushrooms. The local species is a cousin of the Japanese variety, but it is generally larger in stature and tends to have a brown tinge to its cap.

A healthy and growing foraging industry has flourished around the pine mushroom. Pine mushrooms are graded by the age and size of the mushroom. Small, closed buttons are considered the most valuable (Grades 1–3). At this size, the mushroom is considered to be its most aromatic. The texture is also very firm and there is less likelihood of the mushroom being infected with fungus larvae. As the mushrooms mature, their size increases (Grades 4–7) but the value of the mushroom decreases.

This aromatic mushroom attracts the tiny fungus gnat in full force. It is very rare to find large mushrooms that are free of worms. These large specimens are known as "flags" in the industry as they signal the presence of pine mushroom mycelia and the potential for other, more valuable buttons to be present.

Pine Mushroom, or Matsutake (*Tricholoma magnivelare*) Has a firm, dense flesh and a spicy aroma that is reminiscent of cinnamon. The scent is a key factor in determining the identity of the pine mushroom. Look for the pine mushroom in higher altitudes amid stands of mature Douglas fir and hemlock. At lower elevations, they occur in stands of pine and huckleberry. Locally the mushroom starts fruiting in late September and continues until the first hard frosts (usually about mid-November). Once they have smelled a fresh pine mushroom, many find the scent intoxicating. Unfortunately, this volatile aroma is largely lost when the mushroom is dried or frozen. Pine mushrooms can be used like truffles to infuse flavour into a wide variety of dishes.

Caution: Poisonous Look-Alike! Smith's Amanita (*Amanita smithiana*): This species is very similar in appearance (as a small button) to the pine mushroom but its odour is not spicy. The mushroom can be pure white or can have powdery scales on top. There is a shaggy fringe along the edge of the cap and extending to the veil under the cap. It is also an imposing mushroom that can be up to 8 inches (20 cm) tall. The spores and spore print are white.

Best of the Rest: Assorted Fungi

Angel Wing (*Pleurocybella porrigens*) Medium-sized, thin, fan-shaped mushrooms that grow on deadfall almost all year long. They favour forests with hemlock trees and abundant rotted materials on the forest floor. These delicate mushrooms are very fragile and can be easily crushed if you are not paying close attention to your cargo. Angel wings dry very well and have a subtle nutty flavour. In 2004, there were reports of 13 deaths in Japan from people who had consumed angel wings. They were all reported to have had kidney disease but the cause of death was not confirmed. Exercise caution with this mushroom and avoid it if you have kidney or liver issues. Only eat in small quantities.

Bleeding Milk Cap, or Red Juice Milk Cap (*Lactarius rubrilacteus*) Common forest mushrooms that are easy to identify because they exude orange-red juice (or latex) when cut. As the mushroom ages, this juice may take on a greenish hue. The outer flesh tinges green when bruised.

The mushroom is often confused with the false saffron milk cap (*L. deterrimus*), which is the North American equivalent of the *L. deliciosus*, a common culinary delight of Europe and Russia. Russians preserve the mushrooms in salt and consume with shots of vodka. There are a wide variety of *Lactarius* mushrooms out there. Many are not considered prime targets for the forager, as they are frequently riddled with worms. Some have a distinct peppery flavour. Most appear to be harmless.

Button Mushroom, or Field Mushroom (various *Agaricus* species) Similar to the store-bought, common white button mushroom, wild field mushrooms are abundant and an excellent find. Be very careful to distinguish the mushroom from the entire *Amanita* family. If there is any doubt, do not consume the mushrooms. Many poisonings are the result of confusion around these two mushroom families. Make sure the gills are pink or chocolate coloured, not white or yellow. Look for field mushrooms in grassy meadows, particularly where animals are grazing. (That said, beware of *Agaricus* mushrooms in the forest or at the edge of fields.) The undercap of the button mushroom should be pink when young, changing to chocolate brown as the mushroom matures.

Caution: Poisonous Look-Alikes! Destroying Angel (*Amanita ocreata*) and Death Cap (*Amanita phalloides*): Young *Amanita* buttons look similar to young *Agaricus* mushrooms. *A. ocreata* is native to the Pacific Northwest and contains deadly amatoxins. Initial symptoms are vomiting and intestinal issues that last two to three days. Unfortunately, internal damage continues and compromises the function of the kidneys and liver for the next five to six days. At this point, coma and kidney failure are likely. Organ transplants are the only remedy. The *A. ocreata* is rare in British Columbia, but *A. phalloides* is a European species that has been introduced into North America and does poison people. It has an olive-green hue to the cap. When young, *Amanitas* appear egg-shaped and are covered by a thin veil of tissue. There are also other *Amanitas* to be careful about.

Candy Cap, or Western Candy Cap (*Lactarius rubidus*) A small (two inch [5 cm]) mushroom with a reddish-orange cap. It exudes whitish latex and has a

COUNTERCLOCKWISE FROM TOP: LARGE PINE BUTTON, CAULIFLOWER FUNGUS, FIELD MUSHROOMS

sweet scent, reminiscent of maple syrup and caramel, particularly when dried. The cap should not be viscous or slippery, nor should it ever stain yellow when bruised. The stem is smooth (though there may be a little orange fuzz near the base), brittle, and not fibrous. A good mushroom for drying, and often made into cookies and candies by foragers.

Cauliflower Fungus (*Sparassis crispa*) A unique, large fungus that looks like a compact bunch of ribbons. Though not common, it is an excellent find, particularly since one mushroom may weigh several pounds. The aroma is very appealing and the crisp texture makes it one of the best edible mushrooms. Look for the fungus growing at the base of rotting Douglas fir stumps. The mushroom is best fresh, but it does preserve well in sauces or soups. (Before using, soak the whole mushroom in a solution of cold water and salt to rid it of any insect visitors.)

Fairy Ring Mushroom, Mousseron, or Scotch Bonnet (*Marasmius oreades*) Another mushroom to be approached with caution. The mushroom cap is small, less than two inches (5 cm) in diameter. Fairy ring mushrooms are present in grass and in the forest, and tend to grow in arcs or rings. However, there are many other mushrooms that share similar properties, and some are quite toxic. The gills are rather well separated and tan to white in colour. They stop at the stem, or may even stop before reaching the stem. Sometimes the fungus has a faint almond odour. The fairy ring is a sweet mushroom that contains a sugar called "trehalose," the same sugar that makes some insects very sweet to the taste. It dries very well and makes a great mushroom powder.

Caution: Poisonous Look-Alikes!

Ivory Funnel (*Clitocybe dealbata*): A poisonous fungus also known as the "sweating mushroom" from the symptoms it causes. It is funnel-shaped with a depression in the middle of the cap. There is little to no odour. The spore print is white and the gills extend down the stalk, unlike on the *Marasmius*.

False Champignon (*Clitocybe rivulosa*): A small mushroom, one to two inches (2.5–5 cm) in diameter. The cap will have concentric rings of cracks, which expand with age. The rim is often a paler colour. The gills are white with specks of pink.

Hedgehog Mushroom, or Pied de Mouton (*Hydnum repandum*) At first glance, it looks like a large chanterelle but the underside of the cap has a shredded appearance resembling a tiny shag carpet. The flesh is firm and dense, and it is quite delicious in soups or stews. It makes a good dried mushroom. Look for hedgehogs in the same terrain as chanterelles. They tend to like the bottom of valleys and vales, particularly if there is water nearby.

Lobster Mushroom (*Hypomyces lactifluorum*) A vivid red-orange mushroom, this fungus is a joint effort between a host mushroom (usually a *Russula brevipes* or R. *cascadensis* in our area) and a parasite that attacks and transforms the host into an excellent edible mushroom. Guides warn that host mushrooms can be poisonous, so pickers should identify surrounding mushrooms to identify the host. The lobster mushroom has a fluorescent orange, crusty exterior and a firm, sweet flavour. The host mushroom is usually a large, white, gilled mushroom before its transformation.

Oyster Mushroom (*Pleurotus* sp. but usually *P. ostreatus*) Typically white to light-grey, it is a fan-shaped mushroom that grows on dead deciduous trees (usually alder locally). The mushroom grows in clumps on broken trees and on deadfall near the banks of streams and rivers. The oyster mushroom is a good mushroom for the beginning forager because it is abundant and relatively safe to collect.

Parasol Mushroom (*Macrolepiota procera*) **and Shaggy Parasol** (*Chlorophyllum rhacodes* or *C. brunneum*) Very similar mushrooms that appear in similar habitats. The parasol appears in temperate climates all over the planet. They are fairly reliable mushrooms to forage, but caution must be exercised by the beginning forager since there are poisonous mushrooms out there that can be confused by the inexperienced.

Parasols tend to fruit in groups, often in fairy rings or arcs. The true parasol (*Macrolepiota*) is the larger of the two and can reach diameters of up to 16 inches (40 cm). The cap has a characteristic "snakeskin" pattern of scaly flakes. Young buttons are shaped like dense eggs and should have white or pink-tinged gills.

The shaggy parasol has flesh that colours red when cut. Some people have an allergic reaction to the shaggy parasol. Both mushrooms (and, in fact, almost all mushrooms) should not be eaten raw. Eat only a small portion the first time you try these mushrooms and watch for allergic reactions (itching, headaches, etc.). When mature, the mushrooms are fragile and should be handled with care and consumed soon after picking.

Caution: Poisonous Look-Alike! False Parasol (*Chlorophyllum molybdites*): Looks similar to the parasol but will have green spores and a greenish tint to its gills when mature. Young mushrooms are very difficult to distinguish from edible species. The false parasol often appears on lawns and near human activity. It is rare in the Pacific Northwest but common in other areas. Symptoms of poisoning are severe vomiting, diarrhea, and stomach cramps occurring one to three hours after ingestion. Symptoms generally last for up to six hours of unpleasantness. It is one of the most commonly eaten poisonous mushrooms in North America.

The Prince (*Agaricus augustus*) A large *Agaricus* that starts out as a square "marshmallow-shaped" cap, then opens up and becomes almost flat as it matures. There will be a veil covering the young gills, which are pink. Later, the gills will darken to chocolate brown. Distinctive features are a strong almond scent and the sturdy nature of the mushroom. The mushroom will not stain yellow when cut. It is an excellent mushroom for sautéing and makes a wonderful risotto.

Caution: Poisonous Look-Alike! Yellow Staining Agaricus (*Agaricus xanthodermus*): Looks very similar to the prince but has an unpleasant odour and stains yellow when bruised or cut.

Shaggy Mane, or Lawyer's Wig (*Coprinus comatus*) A common mushroom on lawns and in civilized areas. Appears as a white cylinder before it opens up into a more bell-shaped cap. The cap has scales that appear "shaggy" as the mushroom matures. The gills turn black and "auto-digest" (turn into an inky black ooze) to help distribute the spores. The mushroom must be eaten young and does not transport or store well. It has components that do not react well with alcohol, causing nausea, drowsiness, and headaches, and the two should not be consumed together.

Western Sulphur Shelf, or Chicken of the Woods (*Laetiporus conifericola*) A

CLOCKWISE FROM TOP: LOBSTER MUSHROOM, PRINCE MUSHROOM (PHOTO BY SINCLAIR PHILIP), CAULIFLOWER FUNGUS, AMANITA MUSCARIA (PHOTO BY STEPHEN LETTS)

spectacular fungus that grows on deciduous trees. It can be many years old. The eastern cousin is the more familiar *L. sulphureus* (found in most guides). Orange on top and sulphur yellow underneath, it is unmistakable. Only the edges of new growth are tender enough to eat. Mature specimens acquire a strong pungent aroma and a coarse woody texture, making them unacceptable for eating. The fungus has caused digestive upsets in many people. When mature, it has a cardboard-like texture. It has been used as a medicinal mushroom in Asia for centuries. It shows antibiotic properties and apparently has the ability to inhibit the growth of some nasty bacteria (like staphylococcus).

Wood Blewit, Blewit, or Blue Foot (*Clitocybe nuda*) The wood blewit is another mushroom that I include with some caution. It is a mushroom with a fairly wide variety of appearances. Most have a tan cap and a purple- to lilac-tinged stalk. There are *Cortinarius* mushrooms that look similar and some are considered poisonous. The wood blewit is a mushroom that can be cultivated and is occasionally available in the markets or as cultivation spawn (seeded medium). The taste is fairly good with a pleasant aroma. The mushroom holds up well in cooking. The attractive colours fade, however, when the mushroom is cooked. There have been many allergic reactions reported with this mushroom, and it is one that should never be eaten raw.

Caution: Poisonous Look-Alike! Purple Cortinarius (*Cortinarius* sp.: several purple and lilac specimens) and *Inocybe lilacina* (a lilac-coloured variant of *I. geophylla*): These mushrooms have reddish or brown spores, while the blewit has white to pale pink spores. The *Cortinarius* will also have a rust veil on the gills that is sometimes also remnant on the stem. The *Inocybe* has a peaked cap with a fibrous, silky texture.

Truffles

The truffle is the fruiting body of an underground fungus. The term "truffle" can refer to any member of the genera *Tuber*, *Terfezia*, and *Leucangium*. There are also many kinds of false truffles that resemble the ones we eat, but very few have redeeming culinary features and some are even poisonous. Truffles have been around for at least 300 million years (based on fossilized spores found in Piedmont, Italy). In the Middle Ages, truffles turned from being a peasant food to the food of royalty. Their pungent flavour, reputed aphrodisiac properties, and medicinal benefits were held in high esteem. The rarity of the truffle contributed to the allure, and they have become expensive and highly sought after morsels.

Truffles have been found in Europe, Asia, North Africa, and North America, but only three species are commercially important: the white truffle, the black winter truffle, and the summer truffle. All were originally found in Europe but have been successfully cultivated in several places on the planet. Additionally there is a white truffle native to the Pacific Northwest that is gaining in popularity and commercial importance. The fruiting bodies of the truffle occur underground and form a close mycorrhizal association with the roots of specific trees. Truffles are roughly round, warty, and irregular in shape, and vary in dimension from the size of a walnut to that of a small melon. The truffle season for the northern hemisphere falls between September and June. In the southern hemisphere, the season is June to September. Tasmania (Australia) has become a prime region for producing truffles, and their products can rival those of Italy and France.

There are two ultra-famous truffle-producing regions. The first is the Périgord region of France, home to the black or Périgord truffle (*Tuber melanosporum*). It's the truffle of French culinary stardom, used for making pâté de foie gras and many other delicacies. Equally renown is the Italian Piedmont district, home to the white truffle (*Tuber magnatum*), centred in the city of Alba in the northern region of Italy.

Truffles are often cultivated in groves of chestnut, hazelnut, and oak trees. Around 80 percent of the truffles found in France come from specifically planted truffle groves. Although many places in the world are capable of growing truffles, it takes a certain optimum climate to allow the truffle to ripen to its full aromatic potential.

Truffles are often harvested with the aid of truffle dogs that are able to detect the strong smell of mature truffles underneath the surface of the ground. The Italians have developed a specific breed called Lagotto Romagnolo, an ancient breed of water retriever that has been specialized into a truffle-hunting dog. Female pigs have also been used, as they have excellent senses of smell.

However, their use has fallen out of favour as they are difficult to control and tend to eat the truffles before they can be wrestled away by the handler. Another old-school truffle-hunting tip is to look for truffle flies hovering over a ripe truffle near the base of suitable trees. Once a truffle-producing tree is discovered it can be visited and harvested year after year. A typical truffle-bearing tree can produce for up to 30 years. In the Pacific Northwest, the Douglas fir is a host for many types of truffles.

The aroma that helps us find the truffle is also key to its charm and value. The chemicals necessary to develop the aroma are created only after the spores are mature enough for release. Truffles reproduce by means of fungivores (animals that eat fungi). It makes sense, therefore, that the aroma peaks when the truffle has ripened and is ready to produce spores.

In the Pacific Northwest, Oregon is a centre for the harvesting of wild truffles. The white truffle (*Tuber gibbosum*, or *T. oregonense*) is the most significant, but there are also black and brown truffles that are occasionally available in the marketplace. Several pilot projects to establish a commercial truffle cultivation industry on Vancouver Island and in other regions of southwest British Columbia are also underway. Similar initiatives are taking place on the east coast of North America, from the Carolinas all the way up to Quebec. These truffle cultivation efforts may herald new sources of truffles coming our way.

The truffle world is rife with fraud and substandard products, sold to the unsuspecting and sometimes gullible public. Once you have tasted a truffle straight from the ground you know how beautiful and special the experience can be. Most commercially available truffles rarely achieve this level of intensity. The truffle begins to lose volatile elements as soon as it is harvested, so it must be brought to market quickly for the best results. The best truffles are often consumed locally and the rest exported. You can get good truffles in many parts of the world, but the best are eaten soon after harvest and close to the source.

Truffles are also found in North Africa and the Middle East. In the desert after a rainfall, foragers collect black and brown terfez (*Terfezia* sp.). In Islamic culture these truffles are considered a blessing from Allah. They are also considered to be a good tonic for eyesight issues and are renowned as an aphrodisiac. Truffles have been linked with pleasure, privilege, and power from the moment they were first discovered.

In the Pacific Northwest, we are fortunate to be able to forage for the Oregon white truffle. Southern British Columbia is the northern limit of these beautiful nuggets. Locally they are harvested in the early spring, near the base of Douglas fir trees, and are a very exciting find for the lucky forager.

PRESERVING THE HARVEST

Wild mushrooms are a seasonal product, which means they arrive during a short window of time and, occasionally, in a bountiful manner. If you find one beautiful porcini, you are probably going to immediately sauté and eat it with a glorious sense of fulfillment and smug pride (at least that's how I feel!). If you find a large field of porcini, you are going to want to preserve the harvest (and that blissful feeling) for as long as possible.

In the Field

Mushrooms are perishable and begin to deteriorate the moment you pick them. The more delicate the mushroom, the faster its deterioration. Your first considerations should be sustainability and conservation. Ask yourself two questions:

Do you really need to pick that mushroom?

How can you ensure there will be mushrooms in this location in the future?

Mushrooms are the fruit of a much bigger organism, and their main job is to produce spores to help the plant reproduce itself. I usually forage for mushrooms that are relatively plentiful (like the ones described in this book). If you find a large patch of mushrooms, resist the urge to pick every specimen. For one thing, there will usually be a wide range of quality in the mushrooms. Young buttons will not have had time to develop a depth of flavour. Older mushrooms will be starting to decay and may be riddled with worm larvae. I tend to high-grade mushrooms in the field and take only the best, making sure to leave some behind.

If you include wormy mushrooms in your harvest, beware, as the larvae will migrate to other mushrooms during transport and storage. This is particularly important to keep in mind with porcini and pine mushrooms.

There is much debate over the correct way to harvest mushrooms. In a mossy forest floor habitat, it is best to gently push the mushroom at the base of the stalk and pull it up from the forest floor. At that point, you can trim any dirt from the base and clean off as much debris as possible. Never allow dirt to enter your collecting basket or bag. You can use baskets or cloth or even recycled plastic bags while harvesting, as long as you immediately place the mushrooms in a packing basket (a mesh-sided container or wicker basket will do nicely) when you return to your vehicle. If you store mushrooms in a plastic bag, they will sweat moisture and the decaying process will be accelerated.

Other mushrooms (such as the oyster mushroom and the cauliflower fungus) occur on the trunks and stumps of trees and must be cut off with a knife as you harvest them. Oyster mushrooms are fragile, so use a basket for collecting these specimens. A bag would jostle and crush the delicate flesh.

Keep mushroom types separate. However, don't worry too much about the similar cousins like hedgehogs, chanterelles, etc. These varieties you can sort out back home. If there are fragile mushrooms, you can place them in a paper bag to keep them apart in your collecting basket. If you are unsure about the identity of a mushroom, it is a good idea to keep it separated until it can be identified with certainty (i.e., using a guide book or another expert opinion).

Sorting and Airing

Back home, lay newspapers on a table and spread out your collection. Go through the mushrooms to confirm your identifications, discarding any that you are unsure of. You also have a second opportunity to clean the mushrooms, trimming off any brown edges. Check for worms (and worm trails) and discard any specimens that show signs of worms. If the mushrooms are very wet (like chanterelles tend to be) you can leave them out for several hours. Moisture will evaporate and be absorbed by the newspapers.

Choose a storage container with plenty of side ventilation and line it with paper towels or newspaper. Place cleaned mushrooms inside and top with more paper. You now need to judge the moisture content of the mushrooms.

CLOCKWISE FROM TOP: MOREL DRYING RACK (PHOTO BY ERIC WHITEHEAD), CLEAN CHANTERELLES, PORCINI ON THE CUTTING BOARD, SLICED PORCINI

If they appear dry, sprinkle a little water on top of the paper to keep the mushrooms hydrated. If the mushrooms appear wet, don't add any additional water. Place the cleaned mushrooms in a fridge for storage. If you have a bumper crop, process the mushrooms further, using one of the following techniques.

Drying

Drying mushrooms is the most practical way of preserving your harvest. Almost any mushroom can be dried and reconstituted with good results, but some mushrooms are better than others. Porcini and morels are the best dried mushrooms. Their flavour is concentrated and enhanced by the drying process. Chanterelles are less appealing dried. The drying process removes some of the more aromatic notes from that mushroom and makes the final product very tough and fibrous. Pine mushrooms also lose many of the aromatic qualities that make them so highly valued as a fresh mushroom.

Cultivated mushrooms are excellent dried—shiitake, button, and oyster mushrooms in particular. In addition, the medicinal properties of mushrooms will survive the drying process and will be just as potent as in the fresh ones. One of my key techniques for mushroom cooking is to further process dried mushrooms into a powder, which allows you to infuse mushroom flavour into a vast and almost infinite combination of foods (see p. 73).

For home drying, I use a purpose-built dehydrator (mine is an Excalibur brand). It is essentially a small box (the size of a large microwave) with racks, a small heat source, and a fan to allow an even flow of air. Fill the dehydrator with sliced mushrooms in the evening and they will be dry the following morning. Dry until the mushrooms are fairly brittle, but with a slight bend. As the mushrooms cool, they will crisp up and harden. You can also place the mushrooms on a cooling rack and place in a warm oven set to the lowest temperature. You can even set up a drying rack over a water heater or near a wood stove with good results. It will usually take 12 to 18 hours to dry the mushrooms using these makeshift methods.

Freezing

Freezing is an excellent way to preserve many types of mushroom. My freezer is typically loaded up with firm porcini mushrooms, small pine mushrooms, chanterelles, and even morels. Simply place cleaned and dried mushrooms in plastic bags and freeze. Zip-lock freezer bags work well, but for an extended shelf life, vacuum pack the mushrooms (there are many home devices, like FoodSaver or VacMaster, available for this purpose).

Many mushrooms can be frozen whole, or cooked in fat (butter, olive oil, duck fat, etc.) and then frozen. The fat helps preserve some of the more volatile elements of the flavour. You can also make sauces (tomato is my "go to" sauce), soups, or chowders in bulk and freeze them for several months with excellent results. See also Frozen Mushrooms (p. 73).

Pickling

Pickling is the third prime tool for preserving your fungi harvest. There are important rules to follow when canning foods since the process can create an anaerobic environment, which essentially means "without the presence of large amounts of oxygen." Consequently canned foods provide a prime environment for nasty spores like botulism to flourish. The anaerobic process is not all bad, though. It's also responsible for fermentation, which gives us wonderful products like dill pickles and kimchi. These products usually rely on salt (sometimes with the help of chilies) to moderate the levels of harmful bacteria. Unfortunately there have been well-documented cases of mass poisoning from home-canned mushrooms (particularly ones canned in oil and with garlic, a natural carrier of botulism spores). Improper canning can result in serious illness and even death in extreme cases.

Pickling with salt, vinegar, and sugar, however, is a relatively safe method of preservation. That said, it is still a complicated process, so please consult a good modern canning resource like bernardin.ca or freshpreserving.com for more details. The pickle recipes in this book (p.105) are meant to be stored in the fridge and consumed quickly, which eliminates many of the issues with canning.

Infusions

An infusion is the steeping of a substance in liquid to extract culinary or therapeutic properties. This technique has been used since the dawn of civilization with soups, teas, and elixirs. You can use water, alcohol, oil, or fat (butter, duck fat, etc.) to extract many flavour and medicinal components. When you reconstitute dried mushrooms in water, you are making an infusion from that mushroom. This water can be added to stock to magnify its flavour, nutrients, and health benefits.

Alcohol

A current hot trend called mixology has bartenders making mushroom infusions with alcohol to create wildly flavoured cocktails. This is not a new trend: the Japanese have been infusing sake with pine mushrooms for many years. The process is fairly simple and I have included a few recipes (p. 259) to make you a myco-mixologist.

Alcohol is also used to preserve truffles (usually brandy, cognac, or port) and can be purchased commercially. It helps to preserve the flavour of the truffle blended with the flavour of the spirit used. The texture of the truffle is rubbery but the flavour can be quite excellent. (See Truffle Preserved in Cognac, p. 43)

Truffles

The strength of a truffle's aroma is strongly linked to the flavour of its flesh, which will unfortunately start to deteriorate the moment it's picked. Plan to use a truffle the same day you buy it, or at least within several days. Black winter truffles should be used within several days of purchase. Summer truffles will last a couple of weeks longer. White truffles are the most perishable and should be used or processed as soon as possible.

To store temporarily, wrap truffles in damp paper towel and place in a sealed container. Change the paper towel every two days. Your fridge will smell strongly of truffle if you keep truffles in it for more than a few hours. You can also place the truffles in a jar of rice to infuse the flavour into the rice while you wait to cook it. Watch for white mould forming on truffles.

Truffles can also be frozen for months, but use within several weeks for the best results. The texture will be softer if you defrost the truffle, and it may be difficult to slice thinly. Grate or slice partially frozen truffles for the best results. For the highest and best use of your truffles, make one of the following preparations with any leftover truffles.

- **Truffle Butter**—Fat is a very good way to trap the aromatic components of truffles. Finely grate a fresh truffle and add it to softened butter. Let stand at room temperature for an hour. Seal tightly and use with a few days. Truffle butter freezes well for up to one month. You could also add truffles to one of the mushroom compound butters (p. 98) with excellent results. Use within several days or freeze for up to one month for best results.
- **Truffle Honey**—Honey is another excellent medium in which to preserve the aroma of truffles. Heat honey over low until liquid. Grate fresh truffle into the honey, stir well, and place mixture in a glass jar with a tight-fitting lid. The honey will keep almost indefinitely.
- **Truffle Salt**—Salt is one of nature's best preservatives and it makes a great condiment with the addition of grated truffle. Use a good-quality, fine-grained sea salt and grate fresh truffle into the salt. Stir to mix and place in a sealed glass container. The salt will keep indefinitely.
- **Truffle Preserved in Cognac**—Place a washed truffle in a jar and top with cognac (or port). Cover tightly and store in the fridge. The preserved truffle can be kept for several months. The texture of the truffle will be rubbery and the colour will darken considerably. Most of the flavour will be in the cognac. Both the cognac and the truffle can be used to flavour sauces, pâtés, and dishes like risotto and polenta.

Cauliflower fungus Sparassis Crispa
Chicken of the Woods
King Bolete (Porcini)

SHOPPING FOR MUSHROOMS

The number of mushrooms available in our markets is rapidly expanding. Sometimes it is driven by demand for fresh culinary mushrooms (like shiitake and oyster), other times for medicinal mushrooms like Lions Mane and Cordyceps which are available as supplements (capsules, tinctures, tea, coffee substitutes). Supermarkets are now tapping into the trend, and we are seeing mushrooms (both locally grown and imported) becoming very popular in the shops.

The source of mushrooms is always important to identify. For me local is always better. Like any food product, fresh mushrooms can deteriorate over time. The distance from harvest point to store is important. A closer source usually indicates a fresher product.

GENERAL ADVICE

Freshness is the key to buying the best mushrooms, so shop at stores that have a high turnover of product or go to local farmers' markets to get product fresh from foragers and growers.

Here are several simple guidelines:

The mushrooms should appear dry, plump, and free of cracks. Try to avoid mushrooms with browned edges or wrinkles on the cap, or ones that appear saturated with moisture.

Check under the cap of button mushrooms and look for pink or chocolate brown gills. Avoid mushrooms with black gills.

White mushrooms should be evenly coloured and white to creamy in colour. Avoid mushrooms with excessive browning or signs of bruising.

The aroma should be mild; avoid any mushrooms that smell musty or fishy.

Avoid any mushrooms wrapped in plastic that appear to be sweating moisture. Also avoid any mushrooms that show signs of mould growth.

COMMON VARIETIES

Button Mushroom, White Mushroom, or Champignon de Paris (*Agaricus bisporus* var. *albidus*) Button mushrooms are one of the earliest Western cultivated mushrooms, dating back some three hundred years to France. Originally this mushroom was a light-brown colour. Selective breeding of mushroom cultures has developed the pure white specimens we see today. Commercial mushroom farming is now a big business, and the industry has grown very efficient in the art and science of growing and shipping mushrooms. Button mushrooms are a good source of Vitamin D as well as sodium, potassium, and phosphorus. There has been much recent research into the presence of antioxidants and other immune-system-boosting components in these morsels. Raw mushrooms are slightly toxic due to the presence of carcinogenic compounds, which are rendered fairly benign through heating and cooking.

Buy mushrooms that are plump, white, and free of surface blemishes. Buttons that have a thin, white veil covering the gills will last longer than mushrooms with open gills. As the mushroom matures, the gills darken from light pink to dark brown. A pronounced "fishy" smell will indicate that the mushroom is overripe and should be discarded. Place buttons in a paper bag, to allow maximum circulation of air, and store in a fridge. Use within two to three days of purchase.

Brown Button, Cremini, Portobellini, or Portobello (*Agaricus bisporus* var. *brunnescens*) Many stores now carry a brown version of the common button mushroom. These mushrooms are dense and flavourful. The small buttons are marketed as brown buttons or cremini. When allowed to mature to open, mid-sized mushrooms, they are called portobellini. The large, mature specimens are sold as portobellos. These mushrooms are very similar to the white button mushroom in nutritional and medicinal properties and can be used interchangeably in any recipe.

Buy portobello mushrooms that have pink or brown gills. Overripe mushrooms have black gills, strong flavour, and a mild "fishy" odour. In general, the texture of the brown button is superior to the common white button. The flesh is firm, and the mushroom holds its dense shape when cooked. Store mushrooms in a paper bag in the fridge and use within one to two days of purchase. The smaller (unopened) sizes often last up to five days with little drop off in quality.

Enoki Mushroom, Enokitake, Golden Needle, or Velvet Foot (*Flammulina velutipes*) Enoki are commonly available as fragile, sprout-like mushrooms sold in vacuum packages. The mushrooms are highly perishable once the package is opened. The vacuum packaging helps prolong their shelf life and makes them stable for transport. This mushroom has been cultivated in Japan for over three hundred years. The flavour of the mushroom is mild and nutty and is a great last-minute addition to soups and stir-fries. Enoki are also used as medicinal mushrooms in Asia, where they are believed to help improve the immune system. They have also been associated with anti-cancer properties. Enoki mushrooms can now sometimes be found in larger groceries stores and in Asian, specialty, and health food stores.

Oyster Mushroom, or Abalone Mushroom (*Pleurotus ostreatus*) The oyster mushroom is a very fascinating mushroom and one of the most widely

cultivated varieties in the world. Oysters are found in temperate and tropical climates, so they are very well distributed around the planet. Cultivated mushrooms are available in many colours, including white, yellow, brown, and pink. The flesh is fragile and has a slight bitter edge when raw, but which fades after cooking. The mushroom cooks very quickly and should be lightly sautéed or added near the end of cooking. Oyster mushrooms are fungi with reputed immune-system-boosting and anti-cancer properties. There are also studies underway linking oyster mushrooms with the reduction of blood cholesterol levels. Oysters mushrooms also have many fascinating environmental applications. The mushroom's spawn has been used to clean up oil spills, toxic sites, and other persistent ecological ills. These techniques show great potential for these types of environmental remediation.

Oyster mushrooms are best when fresh and plump. As they age, the flesh tends to dry out and crack. Older specimens wilt and may have a pronounced "fishy" odour, so avoid them and buy only fresh, clean-smelling mushrooms. Store oyster mushrooms in a paper bag or in a mesh container covered with a damp paper towel.

CLOCKWISE FROM TOP: ENOKI, MAITAKE, OYSTER

King Oyster, King Trumpet, French Horn, or Cardoncello (*Pleurotus eryngii*) Native to the Mediterranean and the Middle East, this mushroom was introduced to Japan in the early 1990s and its popularity has spread around the globe. The texture of the mushroom is very firm. The king is a very good mushroom for storage and keeps well when refrigerated. The mushroom is reputed to be good for boosting the immune system.

Maitake Mushroom, or Hen of the Woods (*Grifola frondosa*) A popular Japanese mushroom that is now cultivated in North America. It is a fairly firm mushroom that must be cooked to be considered palatable. The mushroom has a place of honour in traditional Japanese and Chinese medicine and is reputed to be beneficial as a total body tonic, boosting the immune system. It has also been indicated for such widely varying benefits as lowering blood pressure and blood sugar levels, and it has shown some modifying effects on the growth of cancerous cells.

Nameko Mushroom, or Butterscotch Mushroom (*Pholiota nameko*) A small amber mushroom, often with a gelatinous coating on the cap. The mushroom is extremely popular in Japan where it is often used in stir-fries and miso soups. Nameko are reputed to have immune-system-boosting properties and anti-inflammatory effects. The texture and taste are sometimes a little surprising to those trying the mushroom for the first time, particularly if it has been cooked a long time. In Japan, they are often sautéed and sprinkled with rice vinegar before being served over steamed rice.

Lion's Mane, Pom Pom, Monkey Head, or Yamabushiitake (*Hericium erinaceus*) A white, shaggy mushroom that is fairly common on hardwood trees. They are now cultivated on compressed sawdust. The mushroom has a fine flavour when young; as it ages, it yellows slightly and takes on a subtle shrimp-like taste. The mushroom is renowned as a medicinal mushroom and has been used for centuries. The mushroom is reputed to boost the immune system and lower blood sugar levels. There is current research into its beneficial effects on memory and cognitive ability, including potential anti-dementia properties.

Shiitake Mushroom, Chinese Mushroom, or Black Mushroom (*Lentinula edodes*) Shiitake mushrooms are native to China, Japan, and Korea and have been cultivated for at least 1,000 years. The name in many Asian cultures translates to "fragrant mushroom" due to its strong aroma and flavour. A native of warmer environments, the mushroom needs heat, moisture, and lots of nutrients to produce fruit. The mushroom is normally grown in bags of growing medium inoculated with shiitake spawn. Some producers introduce shiitake spawn into hardwood logs (usually alder, poplar, or maple logs). The logs produce dense, flavourful premium mushrooms marketed as "log-grown shiitake." The stems of the shiitake are very woody and are often discarded. I like to save them in my freezer to add to a mushroom or vegetable stock.

Dry mushrooms have a very intense flavour and are excellent in stew and soups. Asian cultures place a premium on dry shiitakes with a cracked white cap, often in a flower pattern. These mushrooms are grown at a lower temperature and are sometimes sold at a great cost. They have a thicker cap, creating a great texture. The thicker cap is also thought to be a sign of good energy or chi in the mushroom.

SHIITAKES

Shiitakes have been used as medicine for centuries. The main effect is a boost to the immune system. They are also used as a general health tonic. A friend of mine who is a naturopathic doctor says that in China eating a plate of shiitake mushrooms is the equivalent of "take two aspirin and call me in the morning"—in other words, the first line of defence for whatever ails you. Lentinan, a compound isolated from shiitake mushrooms, has shown promise as an anti-tumour-growth drug and may help other drugs do their job more efficiently when taken in combination. All that goodness in a great-tasting product.

UNUSUAL TYPES

Shimeji Mushroom, or Beech Mushroom (*Hypsizygus tessellatus*) There are two main varieties commercially grown in North America: bunapi-shimeji (white beech mushroom) and buna-shimeji (brown beech mushroom). Shimeji are becoming increasingly available in our stores and restaurants. These mushrooms are packed with *umami* (the Japanese term for a category of flavour that roughly translates to savoury). They are somewhat bitter when eaten raw, but this bitterness eases when the mushrooms are cooked. The cooked mushroom has a nutty flavour and crunchy texture. The small buttons of the shimeji are usually left whole and make an attractive addition to any stir-fry. The mushrooms are also excellent roasted or grilled.

SHIMEJI

Straw Mushroom, Hed Fang, or Nam Rom (*Volvariella volvacea*) The straw mushroom is a common mushroom in Chinese markets. Most often served unopened ("unpeeled"), the dense balls of mushroom add texture and taste to soups, stews, and stir-fries. They are most often found canned in Asian markets. Imported fresh straw mushrooms are sometimes available in markets in larger cities. Dry straw mushrooms are occasionally available in Chinese markets, but they sometimes have a pronounced "funky" flavour that is an acquired taste to Western palates. Straw mushrooms are believed to have anti-cancer and immune-system-boosting properties.

Wood Ear Fungus, Cloud Ear, or Tree Ear (*Auricularia polytricha*) A valued mushroom in Chinese cooking, crunchy black slices are often found in hot and sour soup. The fungus has been used for centuries as a blood purifier and as a tonic for lung infections and stomach upsets. Recent research has indicated the fungus might be useful in lowering LDL cholesterol levels. It also appears to have blood anticoagulant properties.

Usually available dried, fresh wood ears can occasionally be purchased. A dry wood ear will expand to three to four times its size when soaked in water. The crunchy fungus can be added to salads, soups, and stir-fries. The dried fungi will keep indefinitely.

Stropharia, Garden Giant, or Wine Cap Stropharia (*Stropharia rugosoannulata*) Seldom available in our markets but often seen growing in wood-chip and sawdust piles in many parts of the world. It is often available as a mushroom growing kit. The mushroom is large and can grow to be 8 inches (20 cm) high, with a 12-inch (30 cm) wide cap. It is sometimes called the king stropharia for achieving this majestic statue. It has a good taste, particularly when young, although perhaps with a slight overtone of bitterness on the finish. The fragrant adult mushrooms also attract flies and are readily filled with fly larvae. Try to harvest the mushroom when it is unopened. The mushroom is thought to grow well as a companion plant to corn. The stropharia has the potential to be used in bio-remediation, as it apparently has the ability to filter excess bacteria and nitrogen from the environment and render them inert.

White Cloud Fungus, Silver Ear, or Snow Fungus (*Tremella fuciformis*) This ivory-white fungus is closely related to the wood ear. Chinese chefs often use the white cloud fungus in sweet dessert soups. It is thought to enhance memory. Modern research has explored the ability of the white cloud fungus to enhance blood flow to major organs as well as its immune-system-boosting effects. The dried mushroom should be soaked in water for one hour. The hard, yellowish core should be removed before chopping up the fungus into bite-size pieces. The dried fungus will keep indefinitely.

TRUFFLES AND TRUFFLE PRODUCTS

Buying Truffles

The best advice for buying truffles is "Buyer Beware." Any time a product is shrouded in mystery and commands huge sums of money, there is the danger of fraud lurking. Truffles are available in the wild and in plantations of trees inoculated with the truffle organism. There are highly aromatic truffles that are very expensive, and there are other truffles that look very similar to the untrained eye. These details are exploited by both unscrupulous and merely confused retailers. Either way, the chance of finding joy in a fresh truffle purchase has a whole lot of odds piled against it. There are good truffles out there; they are just a little harder to uncover. Working with established companies who put their reputations on the line is a good place to start, but even they are fooled sometimes.

One worrying development in recent years is the import of cheap truffles grown in China. These truffles vary widely in quality and are sometimes passed off as European truffles (which are several orders of magnitude more expensive and powerful). A second nefarious trend is the development of truffle oils flavoured with artificial aromas (more details follow). Real truffle oil will have the truffle type listed on the ingredients label.

Truffle pastes come closest to replicating the true flavour of fresh truffles. These pastes are expensive and often hard to find (see Resources, p. 267, for options). It is useful to blend truffle paste with real truffle oil to punch up the flavour and mimic the real experience of fresh truffles. If by chance you are wealthy and lucky enough to acquire a good source of truffles, congratulations. Here is an overview of the care and handling these beauties require:

White Truffle, Piedmont Truffle, or Alba Truffle (*Tuber magnatum*) The most famous and expensive truffle available. It is renowned for its pungent aroma and its large size. The white truffle has a globular shape, with numerous depressions on the peridium (outer skin) that make it irregular. The outer surface is smooth and slightly velvety. The colour varies from pale cream to dark cream to slightly greenish. Its trama (flesh) is a uniform white or greyish yellow with thin, white veins. Lower-quality white truffles (see Bianchetto, p. 57) will have milk-chocolate-coloured flesh and a strong garlic aroma. Be aware of these truffles being sold as prime white truffles, which unfortunately happens quite often.

The aroma of a white truffle is pleasantly fragrant and should be devoid of a strong garlic smell (see Bianchetto, p. 57). However, a mild garlic or onion aroma is typically present. This truffle lives in symbiosis with oak trees (when it takes on a dark hazelnut colour), lime trees, poplars, and willows (when it is almost pure white), and is rarely found in combination with other truffles. There may be red marks on the peridium if the truffle is in symbiosis with linden trees. The skin turns a darker brown with age. For the best growing conditions, the soil must be rich in calcium and the undergrowth must be low to maintain a good circulation of air.

Most white truffles are native to the foothills and mountains of northern and central Italy and southern Yugoslavia. Fresh white truffles should be lightly coloured and very brittle. It is possible to shatter a white truffle by dropping it on the floor. Large specimens can weigh as much as a kilogram (2.2 lb), but most are the size of large walnuts. The white truffle is slightly more perishable than the black truffle, and the flavour and aroma will diminish within a week or two of harvesting. The white truffle has a distinctive pepper edge and is often eaten raw. The market cost of these truffles can exceed $3,000/pound. The harvest season is mainly September to December.

Black Truffle, Périgord Truffle, or Norcia Truffle (*Tuber melanosporum* sp.) Equally famous (particularly to the French) is the black truffle, which is deep black with a fairly round structure showing distinctive polygonal warts on the surface. The black truffle has a trama that acquires a blackish shade of purple when fully ripe. There are several subspecies of truffles that differ based on terrain, soil, and symbiotic trees. The black truffle is found in France (mainly the Périgord and Vaucluse regions), Italy (the town of Norcia, in the Umbria region), and Spain. In Italy the black truffle is called the Norcia or sometimes the *tartufo nero pregiato*, which roughly translates to "best black" truffle. The unripe flesh is whitish and darkens as it matures to the purplish-black stage. In general the aroma is intense, perfumed, and fruity. Some regard the black truffle aroma as more refined than that of the strongly aromatic white truffle.

The black truffle favours hilly and mountainous areas in symbiosis with hazelnut and oak trees. It is harvested in Europe from December to March. The black truffle is now widely cultivated in Spain, Australia, the United States, New Zealand, and Canada. It is one of the most valuable truffles and has reached market prices of up to $1,500/pound.

Summer Truffle, or Burgundy Truffle (*Tuber aestivum*) The summer truffle is, on the surface, a similar looking specimen to the black truffle. One difference is a brownish hue to the surface warts. The summer truffle also occasionally reaches big dimensions. It has an aromatic smell, but one that seems to diminish quickly when harvested. The truffle is readily distinguished from the black winter truffle once it is cut. In the flesh of truffles you see veins called gleba. In a black truffle, these veins are dark; in a summer truffle, the veins are dark yellow.

The summer truffle grows both in sandy and clayey soils. It's often used for the production of sausages, pâtés, and sauces. In general it is considered an inferior species relative to the black Périgord truffle, and as a result is worth far less, but still currently costs up to $300/pound.

Native to France, Italy, and Spain, summer truffles are usually at their best in July, but can be found from May to October. This truffle has been established on plantations in Sweden and New Zealand.

Bianchetto Truffle, White Spring, Tuscan, or Marzuolo (*Tuber borchii*) Abundant in the Italian regions of Tuscany, Piedmont, and Marche. It can be confused with the white truffle (*T. magnatum*) because, at a first glance, it shows the same characteristics: irregular, smooth, and off-white in colour (ranging from chestnut to muddy). The difference is that when it ripens, it becomes darker (milk chocolate).

The smell is the main characteristic that distinguishes the bianchetto truffle from the white truffle: soft and pleasant at the beginning, becoming garlic-like and nauseating after some time. It grows in limestone soils, often by deciduous and coniferous trees. The collection period is from January to March. They are often labelled as white truffles in preparations and sold as such to those unaware of the difference. The price of bianchetto truffles is usually one-third the price of white Piedmont truffles.

Black Winter Truffle, or Moss Truffle (*Tuber brumale* sp.) Another truffle often confused with the black truffle. The two share the same habitat and the same type of plant symbiosis. The black winter truffle is brownish black with a slightly warty surface; the skin will tend to flake if brushed (the black truffle is much harder). Inside, the flesh darkens, highlighting the white veins. It smells like nutmeg (or some might say mossy) and is far less aromatic than the black Périgord truffle. Correspondingly its value is about half that of the Périgord truffle.

Oregon White Truffle (*Tuber oregonense* and *T. gibbosum*) The Pacific Northwest is home to several types of truffles with great culinary value. These truffles can be found from the west side of the Cascade Range to the coast from southern British Columbia to northern California.

T. oregonense is generally found from October through February. Its skin is whitish when young, developing orange-brown tints as it matures, and finally becoming caramel brown when ripe. *T. gibbosum* is usually found from February through June. Its peridium begins whitish and becomes pale olive-brown as it matures.

In both species, the texture is quite firm (not spongy), and the interior is white when immature, becoming a marbled smokey brown as the truffle matures. Both species seem to prefer young (15- to 40-year-old) Douglas fir plantations. They fruit near the surface of the soil, nestled among the shallow roots of fir trees. Many Oregon white truffles are picked underripe and then matured under refrigeration.

Oregon Brown Truffle (*Leucangium brunneum*) Only discovered in the early 1990s, this truffle grows in younger Douglas fir forests in the Oregon coast range and western foothills of the Cascades. It has a reddish-brown exterior and a greyish, mottled interior. When mature, the odour can be quite garlicky. They are seldom available in the marketplace.

Oregon Black Truffle (*Leucangium carthusianum*, formerly *Picoa carthusiana*) Oregon also has a native black truffle variety, which is larger (golf ball to baseball sized), and is often found much deeper in the soil than the whites (commonly 4- to 10-inches deep). They are very dark inside and out, and have a very pungent, earthy odour when ripe, which not everyone likes. The flesh of this truffle is dark with white veins.

Chinese Truffles (*Tuber sinense*, *T. indicum*, and *T. himalayense*) Over the past few years, we have seen the presence of inexpensive Chinese truffles in the marketplace. There are three main species found in China, mainly in the Yunnan and Sichuan provinces. The truffles occur in cooler climates, in pine forests at an altitude of 2,000 to 2,500 metres (6,000–7,000 ft). The other area of interest is the foothills of the northern Himalayas.

Merchants tend to lump all of the species together as Chinese truffles. However, the flavour and quality vary greatly from one species to another. But generally, the flavour and texture are inferior to French and Italian truffles. *T. indicum* is recognizable by its brown interior and very fine white veins. *T. himalayense* is similar to *T. indicum*, but with a somewhat finer flavour. (It might take genetic analysis to distinguish the two!) *T. sinense* has a dark brown interior with large ivory veins and is distinctly rubbery and bitter. To the casual observer, these truffles look like more expensive truffle varieties, and there have been documented cases of fraud, including mislabelling and injecting the truffle with truffle aromas. Chinese truffles usually sell at a fraction of the cost of European truffles (sometimes for less than $100/pound)—so there is lots of incentive for the unscrupulous.

Oddball Truffles

Pecan Truffle, or Texas Truffle (*Tuber lyonii*, formerly *T. texense*) Found from New Mexico to the Gulf Coast and up the Eastern Seaboard to the Great Lakes and eastern Canada. Its name is based on the habitat where it was discovered. The truffle is present is a wide range of hosts.

Desert Truffle, or Terfez Truffle (*Terfezia boudieri* or *pfielii* or *claveryi*) Native to northern Africa and the Middle East, these truffles are reputed to be the most heavily foraged on the planet. They appear in the desert following heavy rainfalls and are sometimes called the lightning truffle. The desert truffle is reputed to be a strong aphrodisiac. The flavour is also considered to be strong and persist even after cooking. However, the aroma is described as mushroom-like. It is not even close to resembling the aroma and flavour of the *Tuber* species.

Truffle Oil

Truffle oil is one of the most overused items in the modern chef's pantry. One of the key issues is that not all truffle oil is created equal. The majority of oils in the market are made with artificial aromas. These are synthetic compounds (i.e., chemicals) that mimic the natural esters of the truffle. Be sure to look on the label to ensure that real truffles were used in making the product. Artificially flavoured oils will have the word aroma (or *aromi* in Italian) in the list of ingredients. Truffle oil is very pungent and powerful. It will overpower many dishes, particularly when it is drizzled overtop to finish a dish. I like to use the oil sparingly to flavour dairy-based sauces like béchamel, or to infuse flavour into bland bases like mashed potatoes, polenta, or risotto.

The oil must be pasteurized to ensure that no botulism spores are present in the oil. Due to this, it is not recommended that you make your own oil.

Truffle Pastes

Truffle pastes are an excellent way to inject truffle flavour. They have the benefit of being far cheaper than fresh truffles and are available year-round. The pastes are available in white truffle, black truffle, and winter truffle varieties. White truffle paste is the most intense and most expensive product. These pastes are made from truffle trimmings. Read the label carefully, as commercial pastes are often combined with other mushrooms (like porcini or button) and are sometimes a blend of several truffle types.

Truffle Honey

Fine examples of truffle honey are coming out of France, Italy, and Spain. They offer an excellent preservation of true truffle flavour. The only drawback is that they are sweet. You can drizzle the honey over aged cheeses or mix it with lemon juice or vinegar to create a truffle vinaigrette. Truffle honey can also be used to create unique truffle desserts like truffle ice cream (p. 257) or truffle custards.

Other Truffle Products

You occasionally see other added value-added truffle products in the marketplace, including truffle sauces, truffle carpaccio, truffle tapenades, etc. Like most things in life, though, usually you get what you pay for.

CLOCKWISE FROM TOP: OREGON WHITE TRUFFLE, BLACK SUMMER TRUFFLE, OREGON WHITE TRUFFLE CLOSE-UP

GROWING YOUR OWN

Some mushrooms are relatively easy to grow and others are impossible to cultivate. Mycorrhizal mushrooms, which rely on a complex relationship with living trees and plants, are difficult to replicate in a commercial setting. Saprophytic mushrooms, which rely on decomposition, are far better candidates for home cultivation. The most readily available are shiitakes and oyster mushrooms.

CULTIVATED SHIITAKE MUSHROOM KIT

MUSHROOM KITS

Shiitake mushroom kits are usually sold in two forms. The first is shiitake plugs, which are available to use with hardwood logs. The plugs are inoculated with shiitake mushroom spores. It's a simple process: drill holes in the logs, tap in the plugs, and wait 6 to 12 months for the mushrooms to fruit. This takes a long time, but generates a beautiful flush of mushrooms that will fruit over a long timeframe and produces very high-grade mushrooms. Care must be taken to ensure the mushrooms are kept moist and shaded at all times. If the logs dry out, the shiitake mycelia can be destroyed. The best scenario is to place the logs in a shaded forest area that receives a little sunlight (and warmth) during the day but remains out of direct sunlight for long periods.

INOCULATED WOOD CHIPS

The second option for shiitakes is to purchase an inoculated bag of wood chips (usually hardwood, like alder or maple). This is the easiest and fastest way to grow shiitakes. You can buy the kits online (see Resources, p. 267) or occasionally at local farmers' markets or events like Seedy Saturday (an annual garden growers' event). These kits need a good watering, shelter from direct sunlight, and to be kept warm. They can be grown indoors, in a basement or a greenhouse (under a bench, for example). The kits will fruit in about 30 days and produce several pounds of mushrooms. The spawn can then be reactivated after fruiting by placing it in a fridge for a week or so; the process will be restarted. As such, it is possible to achieve several harvests from the same kit.

You can also purchase inoculated wood chips to scatter in a garden pile of wood mulch, which will (in theory) produce a large bed of mushrooms. The results will vary depending on your local conditions and how healthy you keep the mushroom spawn.

Oyster mushrooms can also be purchased in these kits (both the inoculated bags and scattering chip versions). They will produce less (by weight) than a shiitake kit, but the quality of the oysters is far superior to any I have ever purchased. The product is very plump, firm, and noticeably sweeter than most commercial oyster mushrooms.

Mushroom cultivation is an emerging area and new ideas come to market continually. See the resources section (p. 267) for more info.

Edible mushrooms available for home cultivation

- Shiitake (*Lentinula edodes*)
- Oyster—various colours (*Pleurotus* sp.)
- Maitake (*Grifola frondosa*)
- Portobello (*Agaricus* sp.)
- Reishi (*Ganoderma lucidum*)
- Blewit (*Clitocybe nuda*)
- Lion's Mane (or Pom Pom) (*Hericium erinaceus*)
- Enoki (*Flammulina velutipes*)
- Morel (*Morchella* sp.)
- "Garden Giant" Stropharia (*Stropharia rugosoannulata*)

COOKING TIPS & TECHNIQUES

Mushrooms are a perishable product. When cooking with them, you are always looking to remove flaws first. This is most important for foraged and wild mushrooms. You must often clean the mushrooms to remove dirt and pieces of the forest (like pine needles). Care must be taken to remove any spots of decay and mould in particular as it can sometimes cause allergic reactions. If the mushrooms are very dirty, you may have to rinse them under cold water. If you do this, make sure to cook or process the mushroom quickly. Excess moisture will accelerate decay.

In general, it is best to clean and process your mushrooms quickly after purchasing or harvest. Many of the processes described in this chapter help extend the shelf life of your mushrooms, and the quicker you can complete the prep work, the less product you'll waste and the better the processed products will be.

PORCINI IN A CAST-IRON SKILLET

PREPARATION

Cleaning Mushrooms

There are many fallacies out there about cleaning and preparing mushrooms. You often hear that it is wrong to wash mushrooms; however, this is quite often *not* the case. If the mushroom is firm, it makes little difference if you give it a quick rinse to clean off any debris or surface dirt. To do so, keep the mushrooms whole and rinse them quickly under cold water. Shake off excess water and place the mushrooms on a towel. Chop into slices and use immediately. Mushrooms you can wash include: unopened button mushrooms, shiitakes, pines, lobsters, morels, firm porcini, and cauliflower fungi. Mushrooms you should avoid washing include: sliced button mushrooms, chanterelles, oyster mushrooms, enoki, hedgehogs, fairy rings, and soft boletes.

Washed mushrooms should be used as soon as possible. Washing the mushroom will often speed the decaying process and cause browning on the surface of the mushrooms.

Cleaning Truffles

Remove any soil from truffles just before eating. They may be washed with water and brushed gently. The outside must be immaculate since truffles are used unpeeled. Dry with a paper towel. Often the truffle merchant will have done this step for you.

Chopping Vs. Tearing?

How you choose to prepare mushrooms depends on the dish you are creating and the overall look you are going for. It is common to slice mushrooms into even pieces that will all cook at the same time. You can also take these slices and cut them into strips or cubes, which is particularly useful for sauces and pasta dishes. However, some mushrooms, like chanterelles, are stringy in texture and can more easily be ripped into strips with your hands, which adds a rustic touch to the finished dish. Oyster mushrooms also look attractive when torn into strips before cooking. Experiment with these techniques to explore new textures and presentations in your mushroom cooking.

CHOPPED MIXED MUSHROOMS

SAUTÉING

The key to sautéing mushrooms is determining their moisture content. Mushrooms (and chanterelles, in particular) can absorb a lot of moisture in a wet season. When you sauté mushrooms, liquid will pour out, steaming the mushrooms instead of frying them. There are also natural sugars in mushrooms that caramelize as the mushrooms brown. This process, called the Maillard reaction, is one of the keys to developing great flavours in food. For the best results, you should aim for a nice balance of caramelization and texture. To do this, you need to remove excess moisture from the mushrooms before cooking, or cook them at the highest heat possible.

The best first step is to dry the mushrooms on newspaper for several hours (see Sorting and Airing, p. 39). Use a cast-iron or non-stick pan. Heat the pan over medium-high. Add oil or fat and swirl to coat the bottom of the pan. Heat the oil until almost smoking (actually letting it smoke is bad). Add the mushrooms and immediately toss to coat. Unless they are very dry, the mushrooms will bleed moisture into the pan. Be careful not to allow the mushrooms to scorch (burn). If the mushrooms begin to char, they are dry and you can reduce heat or add a splash of water, stock, or wine. You are looking to gently brown the edges of the mushroom to create the caramel effect. At this point, you can season the mushrooms with salt, pepper, and garlic. Toss to warm the garlic through, then remove from heat and enjoy. Butter, olive oil, and duck fat are all good mediums with which to sauté mushrooms.

ROASTING

Roasting is a great way to evenly brown mushrooms and concentrate their flavours. Chanterelles, porcini, hedgehogs, and most cultivated mushrooms are good candidates for roasting. Roasting will make the mushrooms a little tougher, so make sure you don't use huge chunks of mushrooms. Place mushrooms on a tray and toss with fat (olive oil, butter, duck fat, bacon fat, etc.), then season with

BOLETES IN A FRYING PAN

salt, pepper, and garlic. Place in a 350°F (180°C) oven and roast for about 20 to 30 minutes. Halfway through roasting you can add a few chopped fresh herbs, such as rosemary, sage, or parsley. Toss the herbs to coat with fat and continue roasting until the mushrooms are browned on the edges.

GRILLING

Grilling is suitable for a few mushroom types, particularly porcini, chanterelle, pine, and oyster mushrooms. Shiitake, lobster, and button mushrooms are also very good but tend to char easily. Make sure to grill mushrooms lightly for the best results. Another good technique is to wrap mushrooms in aluminum foil and place the package on the grill. This is particularly good with thicker mushrooms, like portobellos, or delicate mushrooms, like maitake and enoki. Try putting grilled mushrooms in one of the compound butters (like the miso, p. 98) for a wonderful effect.

STEAMING

Steaming is an often-overlooked method for cooking mushrooms. Try it with button or chanterelle mushrooms for an interesting twist. Steaming creates a softer texture but leaves a clean mushroom flavour. Top the steamed mushrooms with lemon juice and olive oil and season well with salt and pepper. You can also drizzle with melted garlic butter or season with light soy sauce.

REHYDRATING

Some mushrooms, like morels and porcini, are considered even more flavourful when dried and reconstituted (see p. 40). Bring these mushrooms back to life by soaking in water. Hot water will speed up the rehydration process. Some mushrooms, morels in particular, have a fine grit that adheres to them, even when dried. As a result, when reconstituted, a fine sediment settles on the bottom of the dish. You can use the soaking liquid to flavour your dishes, but always discard the sediment.

Use the following steps when rehydrating mushrooms:

Place mushrooms in a heatproof container (I like to use a glass measuring cup).

Pour boiling water over the mushrooms and immediately strain through a wire sieve.

Put mushrooms back in the container and cover again with boiling water.

Let stand until cool enough to handle, then remove mushrooms, drain, and chop. Reserve the soaking liquid to add to sauces and soups.

Use the mushrooms and soaking liquid in your favourite recipe.

MUSHROOM POWDER

Dried mushrooms pack a lot of flavour. Grinding them into a powder allows you to take those properties to a whole new level. You can then use the powder to infuse mushroom flavour into many of the recipes in this book. The key to grinding a mushroom into powder is starting with a very dry mushroom.

Previously dried mushrooms tend to reabsorb moisture out of the atmosphere they are stored in. If the mushrooms appear soft and bendable, reheat in a 350°F (180°C) oven for two to three minutes. Allow the mushrooms to cool (they will crisp up as they cool), then use a small, electric coffee grinder (or spice grinder) to make small batches of powder. The powder will keep indefinitely if stored in a tightly closed container. Porcini is the best mushroom to grind, but shiitake, button, and fairy ring mushrooms also make great flavouring powders.

FROZEN MUSHROOMS

When sautéing frozen mushrooms, it is best to cook them when they are still partially frozen. The internal structure of the mushroom is like a sponge: when the mushroom freezes, the expansion of liquid stretches the cells. When the mushroom thaws, the structure collapses and liquid streams out. Along with this liquid, sugars, nutrients, and flavour also exit. Cooking mushrooms semi-frozen allows you to preserve some of their texture and natural sweetness. It also allows the sugars to caramelize on the surface of the mushrooms. Sautéed frozen mushrooms won't be as fine as fresh mushrooms, but they will still be very good.

Slowly defrost the mushrooms if possible. If you place them in the fridge in the morning, they should be just about right for dinner. You can also defrost the mushrooms on the counter for about an hour. If you have frozen whole mushrooms, cook the mushrooms as soon as you cut them. If they are in fat or sauce, simply defrost and use in your favourite recipe. (See Freezing, p. 41).

STOCKS

CULTIVATED MUSHROOM ASSORTMENT

MUSHROOM VEGETABLE STOCK

MAKES 4 QUARTS (4 L)

This is my go to stock for vegetarian dishes and for adding flavour to sauces and soups. Shiitake mushrooms are always in my cupboard and are an excellent source of immune-system-boosting nutrients. These dry mushrooms are also an excellent source of umami for creating and building flavours in anything you cook.

4 quarts (4 L) water
8 large dried shiitake mushrooms
2 cups (500 mL) whole button mushrooms
1 cup (250 mL) peeled and chopped onions
1 cup (250 mL) peeled and chopped carrots
1 cup (250 mL) chopped celery
4 garlic cloves
1 Tbsp (15 mL) chopped fresh rosemary
1 Tbsp (15 mL) chopped fresh sage

1. In a large stockpot, combine all the ingredients. Bring to a boil, reduce heat, and simmer uncovered for 1 hour.
2. Strain the stock into a container and remove the shiitake mushrooms. Discard the rest of the vegetables and the herbs. Cut the stems off the shiitakes and discard. (The shiitake caps can be used in a stir-fry or stew, or may be sliced thinly and returned to the broth.) Place the container on a wire rack and let stock cool until room temperature, then refrigerate in a covered container. Keeps for 3–4 days in the fridge or for up to 3 months when frozen.

QUICK MISO MUSHROOM STOCK

MAKES 4 QUARTS (4 L)

Miso stock is a nutritious stock that can be prepared very quickly. I use strips of kombu about 6 inches (15 cm) long. You may be able to find the same seaweed shredded in Japanese and health food stores. This combination of ingredients is known to boost your immune system and aid your digestive functions.

4 quarts (4 L) water
8 large dried shiitake mushrooms
2 cups (500 mL) whole button mushrooms
½ cup (125 mL) shiro (light) miso paste
1 piece dried kombu (bull kelp) seaweed (about 1 oz [28 g])
4 green onions, chopped
¼ cup (60 mL) dried dashi flakes (or 1 package instant dashi powder)
2 garlic cloves

1. In a large stockpot, combine all the ingredients. Bring to a boil, reduce heat, and simmer uncovered for 1 hour.
2. Strain the stock into a container and remove the shiitake mushrooms. Discard the button mushrooms, seaweed, onions, and garlic. Cut the stems off the shiitakes and discard. (The shiitake caps can be used in a stir-fry or stew, or may be sliced thinly and returned to the broth.) Place the container on a wire rack and let stock cool until room temperature, then refrigerate in a covered container. Keeps for 3–4 days in the fridge or for up to 3 months when frozen.

MUSHROOM BACON STOCK

MAKES 4 QUARTS (4 L)

Bacon makes everything better. You will believe it after making this stock. The smoky perfume of the bacon makes this stock a fantastic base for soups and sauces. Chill the stock after straining and you can skim any fat off the top of the cooled stock.

4 quarts (4 L) water
1 lb (450 g) slab smoked bacon (or smoked ham hock)
8 large dried shiitake mushrooms
2 cups (500 mL) whole button mushrooms
1 cup (250 mL) peeled and chopped onions
1 cup (250 mL) peeled and chopped carrots
1 cup (250 mL) chopped celery
4 garlic cloves
1 Tbsp (15 mL) chopped fresh rosemary
1 Tbsp (15 mL) chopped fresh sage

1. In a large stockpot, combine all the ingredients. Bring to a boil, reduce heat, and simmer uncovered for 1 hour.
2. Strain the stock into a large container, then remove the shiitake mushrooms and bacon slab. Discard the rest of the vegetables and the herbs. Cut the stems off the shiitakes and discard. (The shiitake caps can be used in a stir-fry or stew, or may be sliced thinly and returned to the broth. The bacon can be sliced and added to many recipes.) Place the container on a wire rack and let stock cool until room temperature, then refrigerate in a covered container. Keeps for 3–4 days in the fridge or for up to 3 months when frozen.

CHICKEN MUSHROOM STOCK

MAKES 4 QUARTS (4 L)

A good chicken stock is the secret weapon of any kitchen. The gelatin in the bones is extracted and helps coat the mouth with flavour. The mushrooms add a depth of flavour that is harmonious with the chicken. In commercial kitchens, all of the mushroom stems (including tough shiitake stems) are used to make this stock. The medicinal properties of the mushrooms and chicken make this a potent health-promoting broth.

4 lb (2 kg) chicken back and neck bones
1 cup (250 mL) peeled and chopped onions
1 cup (250 mL) peeled and chopped carrots
1 cup (250 mL) chopped celery
2 cups (500 mL) chopped white button mushrooms
1 handful fresh herbs (sage, rosemary, marjoram, etc.)
2 garlic cloves, chopped
1 tsp (5 mL) salt
4 quarts (4 L) cold water (enough to completely cover the bones)

1. Place the bones in a pot or large bowl and cover with water. Let soak for at least 10 minutes, then drain, rinse with fresh cold water, and drain again.
2. In a large stockpot, add the bones and all the vegetables and seasoning. Cover the bones with the measured cold water. Bring to a boil, then reduce to a simmer. Gently simmer the stock for 1–2 hours.
3. Pour the stock through a strainer into a storage container and let cool to room temperature. When cool, cover and place in the fridge to chill (overnight is best). The fat will congeal on the top and then can be easily removed. The stock should thicken from the gelatin in the skin and bones. Use in your favourite recipe or place in freezer bags and freeze for up to 3 months. There might be a layer of sediment that forms on the bottom of the chilled stock—this is protein and congealed blood and can be discarded.

DUCK MUSHROOM STOCK

MAKES 4 QUARTS (4 L)

I like to roast the bones for my duck stocks; the caramelization of the sugars in the meat along with the gelatin in the bones makes a unique and incredibly delicious broth. Use this stock in place of chicken stock in any of the recipes in this book.

1 duck carcass (back and neck, bones, etc.)
1 cup (250 mL) peeled and chopped onions
1 cup (250 mL) peeled and chopped carrots
1 cup (250 mL) chopped celery
2 cups (500 mL) whole mushrooms (button, chanterelle, oyster, shiitake, etc.)
1 handful fresh herbs (sage, rosemary, marjoram, etc.)
2 garlic cloves, peeled and chopped
1 tsp (5 mL) salt
4 quarts (4 L) cold water (enough to completely cover the bones)

1. Preheat the oven to 350°F (180°C).
2. Place the bones in a pot or large bowl, cover with water, and let soak for at least 10 minutes, then drain, rinse with fresh cold water, and drain again.
3. Place the bones, onions, carrots, celery, and mushrooms on a roasting tray. Place in the oven and roast for 20 minutes, or until well browned but not burnt.
4. In a large stockpot, combine the roasted bones and vegetables. Add the herbs, garlic, and salt. Cover bones with the measured cold water. Bring to a boil, then reduce to a simmer. Gently simmer stock for 1–2 hours, straining off any foam that forms on the surface.
5. Pour stock through a strainer into a storage container and let cool to room temperature. When cool, cover and place in the fridge to chill (overnight is best). The fat will congeal on the top and then can be easily removed. The stock should thicken from the gelatin in the skin and bones. Use in your favourite recipe or place in freezer bags and freeze for up to 3 months. There might be a layer of sediment that forms on the bottom of the chilled stock—this is protein and congealed blood and can be discarded.

BEEF MUSHROOM STOCK

MAKES 4 QUARTS (4 L)

Beef stock is the richest stock in the kitchen pantry. It is the base of many fantastic sauces and is often reduced down to a thick jelly called demi-glace (see p. 85). Roasting the bones is important to develop flavour. Mushrooms add a deep richness to the stock and make a very flavourful broth by increasing the caramel notes in the finish.

4 lb (2 kg) beef bones (shank is best)
Salt and pepper, to taste
1 cup (250 mL) peeled and chopped onions
1 cup (250 mL) peeled and chopped carrots
1 cup (250 mL) chopped celery
2 cups (500 mL) chopped mushrooms (button, shiitake, oyster, etc.)
4 quarts (4 L) cold water (enough to completely cover the bones)
4 Tbsp (60 mL) chopped mixed fresh herbs (rosemary, sage, marjoram)

1. Preheat the oven to 350°F (180°C).
2. Rinse the bones under cold water until the water runs clear. Place in a roasting pan and season with salt and pepper. Place in the oven and roast for 1 hour. Add the onions, carrots, celery, and mushrooms to the bones. Continue roasting for another 30 minutes, or until the vegetables are browned and the bones are well roasted.
3. Transfer to a stockpot, scraping off and adding any brown bits from the bottom of the pan (or deglaze the pan by adding water, wine, or beer to dissolve the bits). Cover the bones with the measured cold water and bring to a boil. Immediately reduce to a simmer and discard any foam that floats to the surface, as it will discolour the stock and add bitter flavours if left in.
4. Add the mixed herbs and gently simmer for 4–6 hours. Remove from heat and let cool. Strain the stock through a wire mesh strainer or colander into a clean storage container. Let the stock cool on a rack to room temperature. Cover with a lid and cool overnight. The next day, remove the layer of fat. The stock will keep for 1 week if refrigerated and up to 3 months if frozen.

LAMB MUSHROOM STOCK

MAKES 4 QUARTS (4 L)

Lamb stock is richly flavoured and is enhanced by the earthiness of the mushrooms. It will even handle stronger mushrooms like shiitake and porcini. If I am trimming older porcini, I like to add the soft sponge of the cap to this stock to punch up the flavour. It is import to chill the stock and remove all the fat, since it can add an overpowering flavour.

4 lb (2 kg) lamb bones
Salt and pepper, to taste
1 cup (250 mL) peeled and chopped onions
1 cup (250 mL) peeled and chopped carrots
1 cup (250 mL) chopped celery
2 cups (500 mL) chopped mushrooms (button, shiitake, oyster, etc.)
4 quarts (4 L) cold water (enough to completely cover the bones)
4 Tbsp (60 mL) chopped mixed fresh herbs (rosemary, sage, marjoram)

1. Preheat the oven to 350°F (180°C).
2. Rinse the bones under cold water until the water runs clear. Place in a roasting pan and season with salt and pepper. Place in the oven and roast for 1 hour. Add the onions, carrots, celery, and mushrooms to the bones. Continue roasting for another 30 minutes, or until the vegetables are nicely browned and the bones are well roasted.
3. Transfer to a stockpot, scraping off any brown bits from the bottom of the pan (or deglaze the pan by adding water, wine, or beer to dissolve the bits). Cover the bones with the measured cold water and bring to a boil. Immediately reduce to a simmer and discard any foam that floats to the surface, as it will discolour the stock and add bitter flavours if left in.
4. Add the mixed herbs and simmer for 4 hours. Remove from heat and let cool. Strain the stock through a wire mesh strainer or colander into a clean storage container. Let the stock cool on a rack to room temperature. Cover with a lid and cool overnight. The next day, remove the layer of fat. The stock will keep for 1 week if refrigerated and up to 3 months if frozen.

DEMI-GLACE

MAKES 1 QUART (1 L)

This heavily reduced stock is called “demi” in the kitchen and is the foundation of most high-end restaurant stocks. It takes a lot of effort to make and is increasingly being replaced by bouillon cubes and powders. You can taste the clean flavours of the beef in the real deal. Traditionally made with veal or beef bones, you can also make a good version with chicken, lamb, or game (venison, elk, buffalo, moose, etc.) bones. Don’t make demi with store-bought stocks, as the usually high salt content will make the final result inedible.

4 quarts (4 L) good strong beef or lamb stock (p. 83 or 84)

1. Remove all fat from the stock, as any fat will make the end result cloudy. Place the stock in a stockpot and boil rapidly until the volume is reduced by three-quarters. The demi will keep for 1 week in the fridge or can be frozen for up to 1 month.

TRUFFLE DEMI

MAKES ABOUT 1 CUP (250 ML)

This technique can be used with any sautéed mushroom. You can also make a delicious variation by using ¼ cup (60 mL) whipping cream in place of the butter. Any number of fresh herbs can also be added at the finish (rosemary, thyme, sage, etc.).

1 cup (250 mL) demi-glace (p. 85)
1 Tbsp (15 mL) sweet sherry
2 Tbsp (30 mL) unsalted butter
Fresh truffles, sliced (as many as you can afford!)

1. Place the demi-glace in a saucepan, bring to a boil, and then add the sherry. Remove from heat and add the butter, swirling to melt the butter gently. The sauce should thicken and become glossy. Add the truffle slices and swirl to mix. Serve immediately.

PANTRY RECIPES

MUSHROOM PASTA

SERVES 4

A simple and excellent pasta recipe. The food processor makes short work of the job of making this pasta. It is also good for making ravioli and lasagna. For a simple meal, boil the pasta and toss it with a little butter, olive oil, and Parmesan cheese.

1 cup (250 mL) all-purpose flour
1 Tbsp (15 mL) mushroom powder (porcini, morel, lobster, etc.) (p. 73)
½ tsp (2 mL) salt
1 egg, beaten
2 Tbsp (30 mL) water

1. In the bowl of a food processor, pulse together the flour, mushroom powder, and salt. Add the egg and pulse again to mix. Add the water 1 tablespoon (15 mL) at a time until the dough comes together in a ball. Remove from the food processor, wrap in plastic wrap, and refrigerate for at least 1 hour.
2. Cut the dough into 2 pieces and run each piece through a pasta machine to make a long thin sheet. Lay each sheet on a flat work surface.
3. Cut the sheets into 1-foot (30 cm) segments and either cut with a knife (or pizza cutter) or use the pasta cutter attachment of the pasta machine to make linguini or spaghetti.
4. Cook pasta in boiling salted water for 3–4 minutes, then drain and serve with tomato mushroom sauce (p. 222).

PORCINI GNOCCHI

SERVES 4–6

These little pillows of potato dumplings are turned into a thing of beauty with the addition of a little mushroom powder. This recipe is excellent with porcini powder, but I have made versions with other mushrooms that turned out very well, including using smoked mushrooms to make the powder. You could also add freshly grated truffle or truffle paste for a special treat.

1½ lb (about 680 g) russet potatoes
1 Tbsp (15 mL) finely minced fresh sage
1 cup (250 mL) all-purpose flour
2 Tbsp (30 mL) porcini powder (or lobster, chanterelle, morel, etc.) (p. 73)
1 large egg
1 pinch salt
¼ cup (60 mL) fresh goat cheese
Olive oil, to coat

1. Boil the potatoes until they are soft, about 45 minutes. While still warm, peel and pass them through a vegetable mill or potato ricer (or, if you don't have one, you can mash the potato with a masher or fork) onto a clean pasta board. Add the sage and lightly mix with a fork.
2. Make a well in the centre of the potatoes and sprinkle flour and porcini powder all over, using up all the flour. Place the egg, salt, and goat cheese in the centre of the well and, using a fork, stir into the flour and potatoes, just as you would when making normal pasta. Once the egg is mixed in, bring the dough together with your hands, kneading it gently until a ball forms. Knead gently for another 1–2 minutes, until the dough is smooth.
3. Roll a fist-sized ball of dough into a ¾-inch (2 cm) diameter rope and then cut into 1-inch (2.5 cm) long pieces. Roll each piece into a ball and flatten slightly with a fork. Place on a well-floured tray. Continue until remaining dough is used up.
4. Bring a large pot of salted water to a boil. Set up a large bowl filled with cold water nearby.
5. Drop gnocchi in batches into the boiling water and cook them until they float, about 1 minute. Remove the gnocchi with a slotted spoon and place in the cold-water bath. Continue until all the gnocchi are cooked. Strain water and drain well. Place gnocchi on a clean tray and toss with oil. Can be refrigerated until needed. To serve, fry gnocchi in butter or olive oil. Top with your favourite sauce (see p. 221 for suggestions) or simply serve with freshly grated Parmesan cheese.

MUSHROOM SPAETZLE

SERVES 4

Spaetzle is a German egg dumpling that is addictive and unusual. You can buy spaetzle makers to create a more uniform dumpling. Traditionally spaetzle is pan-fried in browned butter and sage to crisp up the exterior. The result is spectacular with rich reduced stock sauces and matches well with pork and duck dishes.

1 cup (250 mL) all-purpose flour
1 Tbsp (15 mL) morel powder (or other mushroom powder) (p. 73)
1 tsp (5 mL) sea salt
½ tsp (2 mL) ground pepper
½ tsp (2 mL) ground nutmeg
2 large eggs
¼ cup (60 mL) milk
Olive oil, to coat
3 Tbsp (45 mL) salted butter
2 Tbsp (30 mL) minced fresh chives or sage
Salt and pepper, to taste

1. In a large bowl, combine the flour, morel powder, salt, pepper, and nutmeg. In another mixing bowl, whisk the eggs and milk together. Make a well in the centre of the dry ingredients and pour in the egg-milk mixture. Gradually draw in the flour from the sides and combine well using your hands; the dough should be smooth and thick. Let the dough rest for 10–15 minutes.
2. In a large pot, bring 3 quarts (3 L) of salted water to a boil, then reduce to a simmer. To form the spaetzle, hold a large-holed colander over the simmering water and add the batter. Push the dough through the holes with a spatula or spoon. Do this in batches so you don't overcrowd the pot. Cook for 3–4 minutes, or until the spaetzle floats to the surface, stirring gently to prevent sticking. Dump the spaetzle into another colander and give it a light coating of oil. Transfer to a baking sheet and let cool.
3. In a large skillet over medium heat, melt the butter and then add the spaetzle, tossing to coat. Cook the spaetzle for 1–2 minutes to give the dumplings some colour, then sprinkle with the chopped chives or sage (or both) and season with salt and pepper before serving.

MUSHROOM RICOTTA GNUDI

SERVES 4–6

A gnudi is a dumpling made with cheese as the main ingredient. It can be used like gnocchi but is generally creamier and a little richer in flavour. You can freeze these nuggets on a tray and then repackage for storage. To cook, drop while still frozen into boiling water and remove once they float to the surface. To serve, toss the gnudi in good olive oil and freshly grated Parmesan cheese. You can also use a browned butter sauce with sage and garlic or a tomato mushroom sauce (p. 222) with spectacular results.

1 lb (450 g) fresh ricotta cheese
¼ cup (60 mL) finely grated Parmesan cheese
1 large egg, lightly beaten
2 Tbsp (30 mL) olive oil
Pinch of nutmeg
Salt and pepper, to taste
1 cup (250 mL) all-purpose flour, plus more for rolling
1 Tbsp (15 mL) mushroom powder (porcini, shiitake, morel, button, etc.) (p. 73)
1 cup (250 mL) semolina flour
Parmesan cheese, for garnish

1. In a large bowl, combine the ricotta, Parmesan, egg, olive oil, and nutmeg. Season with salt and pepper and then sprinkle the flour and mushroom powder overtop. Toss lightly with a fork to incorporate the flour. Dust the dough lightly with more flour to make the surface less sticky and then shape into a ball. On a lightly floured work surface, roll the dough out into a rope and cut into 1-inch (2.5 cm) pieces. Gently roll the pieces into balls and transfer to a baking sheet covered with semolina flour. Roll the balls in the semolina and let rest for at least 1 hour in the fridge.
2. Bring a large pot of salted water to a boil, then add the gnudi and cook for about 5–6 minutes, or until they float to the surface and are cooked through. Drain and immediately coat with olive oil (or add to a sauce). If not serving immediately, spread out on a tray and allow to cool. Refrigerate or freeze until needed. Stir gnudi gently to coat with the oil or sauce. Toss to warm through and spoon into serving bowls or onto plates. Top with a sprinkling of fresh Parmesan cheese and serve.

MUSHROOM AÏOLI

MAKES ABOUT 1 CUP (250 ML)

Homemade mayo has been frowned upon in recent years. However, if you use organic free-range eggs, you are reducing the risk of complications dramatically. Even so, be careful if you have a weakened immune system (young, old, pregnant, etc). You can also use a store-bought (pasteurized) mayonnaise and add mushroom powder (or truffle paste) and lemon to produce a similar sauce.

½ tsp (2 mL) minced garlic
1 tsp (5 mL) mustard
1 egg yolk
1 tsp (5 mL) mushroom powder (p. 73) (or truffle paste)
1 cup (250 mL) olive oil (or grapeseed oil)
2 Tbsp (30 mL) lemon juice (or dry white wine vinegar)
Salt and pepper, to taste

1. In a mixing bowl, mash the garlic with the back of a spoon until a paste is formed. Add the mustard, egg yolk, and mushroom powder. Whisk until smooth. Add the oil in a slow steady stream until about half incorporated. Add the lemon juice and whisk until smooth. Add the remainder of the oil in a slow steady stream until fully incorporated. (You can add more oil if you prefer a thicker aïoli.) Season with salt and pepper and refrigerate until needed.

BASIC FLAKY PIE DOUGH

ENOUGH PASTRY FOR 3 LARGE TARTS

A versatile pie dough that works well for desserts or savoury pies. Mixing gently to bring the dough just together makes a very tender and flaky pastry. Freeze any leftover dough for up to one month.

5½ cups (1.375 L) all-purpose flour
2 tsp (10 mL) salt
1 lb (450 g) lard or shortening
1 egg, beaten
1 Tbsp (15 mL) vinegar

1. In a mixing bowl, stir together the flour and salt. Cut the lard or shortening into rough cubes and toss in the flour. Cut in the lard using a pastry cutter or two knives until the mixture resembles pea-sized lumps. In a measuring cup, beat the egg with a fork. Add the vinegar and enough cold water to make 1 cup (250 mL). Stir the liquid into the flour mixture until incorporated and the dough starts to come together. Gently knead until the mixture just comes together in a ball. Cover with plastic wrap and refrigerate for at least 1 hour. When ready to proceed, roll out the dough on a floured work surface, using a good dusting of flour on the dough and rolling pin. Proceed with the directions in the pie recipe. The dough can also be frozen for up to 1 month.

MUSHROOM COMPOUND BUTTERS

MAKES 6–8 SERVINGS EACH

Compound butters are a great way to infuse mushroom flavour into a wide array of foods. They are great on steaks, salmon, grilled mushrooms, baked potatoes, and pastas.

Herb mushroom butter
¼ lb (115 g) butter, softened, divided
1 cup (250 mL) minced mushrooms
1 tsp (5 mL) minced garlic
2 Tbsp (30 mL) minced fresh chives
2 Tbsp (30 mL) minced fresh parsley
1 Tbsp (15 mL) minced fresh sage
Salt and pepper, to taste

Miso mushroom butter
¼ lb (115 g) butter, softened
1 cup (250 mL) minced mushrooms
1 tsp (5 mL) minced garlic
¼ cup (60 mL) shiro (light) miso paste
2 Tbsp (30 mL) minced fresh chives
1 tsp (5 mL) sesame oil
Salt and pepper, to taste

Garlic mushroom butter
¼ lb (115 g) butter, softened
1 cup (250 mL) minced mushrooms
1 Tbsp (15 mL) minced garlic
1 tsp (5 mL) Worcestershire sauce
2 Tbsp (30 mL) minced fresh parsley
2 Tbsp (30 mL) finely shredded Parmesan cheese
Salt and pepper, to taste

1. In a skillet over medium-high heat, add 1 tablespoon (15 mL) of the butter and the mushrooms. Sauté until the mushrooms begin to stick to the bottom of the pan. Remove from heat and let cool slightly.
2. Place the remaining butter in a mixer with a paddle attachment. Mix to soften, then add the sautéed mushrooms, garlic, chives, parsley, and sage. Pulse to mix, then season well with salt and pepper (the amount you use depends on whether or not you used salted butter). Place flavoured butter onto a sheet of plastic wrap, forming a line down the middle. Fold the plastic over and roughly form into a log. Roll up the plastic and twist the ends to form a compact and round log. Transfer to the fridge and chill until firm. Cut into rounds to serve.
3. The following variations use the same technique: miso mushroom butter, garlic mushroom butter.

PORCINI YORKSHIRE PUDDING

MAKES 12 SERVINGS

We love our Yorkshire pudding. It gets trotted out at most family gatherings, even if we are roasting a turkey or a beautiful chicken. If there is gravy on the menu, my family demands the Yorkshire to mop it all up. I hit on the idea of using the mushroom powder early on—in fact, it was the gateway recipe for many other recipe experiments. The duck fat also adds an incredible flavour to the dish. It must be tasted to be believed.

1 cup (250 mL) all-purpose flour
1 Tbsp (15 mL) porcini powder (p. 73)
1 tsp (5 mL) chopped fresh rosemary
Salt and pepper, to taste
1 cup (250 mL) milk
4 eggs
1 cup (250 mL) duck fat (or bacon fat or grapeseed oil)

1. Preheat the oven to 375°F (190°C).
2. In a mixing bowl, combine the flour, porcini powder, rosemary, salt, and pepper. Make a well in the centre and add the milk and eggs. Whisk gently until a smooth batter is formed. Set aside to rest while preparing the baking tins.
3. In a muffin tin, add about 1 tablespoon (15 mL) of duck fat to each compartment. Place on a baking sheet and place in the oven. Heat for 10 minutes; the fat should be quite hot and almost smoking. Pour the batter into the hot fat, filling each tin about three-quarters full. Place in the oven and cook for 20 minutes with the door closed. Do not open the door until the puddings have risen and are firm.

MUSHROOM TEMPURA BATTER

MAKES ABOUT 2 CUPS (500 ML) BATTER

There are a few essential tips to making a good tempura batter. First, use a low-gluten flour like cake flour or all-purpose flour (not bread flour). Second, make sure the soda water is ice cold (I like to place it in the freezer for about 15 minutes prior to using). Third, mix the batter gently. Like making a good pancake mix, leave a few lumps in the batter to ensure lightness. And use the batter up within 30 minutes of mixing—the sooner, the better.

1 cup (250 mL) all-purpose or cake flour
1 Tbsp (15 mL) mushroom powder (porcini, button, shiitake, etc.) (p. 73)
1 Tbsp (15 mL) cornstarch or tapioca starch
1½ cups (375 mL) soda water, ice cold

1. In a mixing bowl, combine the flour, mushroom powder, and starch. You can use chopsticks or a fork to mix the batter. Add the soda and stir gently until the mixture is fairly smooth but with a few small lumps still left. Let stand for about 5 minutes and then use within half an hour.

TAPAS, MEZES, AND PICKLES

TRUFFLE POTATO CROQUETTES

MAKES 24

Makes an elegant appetizer or a side dish for many plates. You can make the balls in advance and fry them at the last minute. You can keep them warm in the oven for up to 30 minutes after frying. As an alternative to frying, the croquettes can be baked in the oven. The balls may collapse slightly but they will still be tasty. Bake until golden brown, about 20 minutes.

4 russet (or baking) potatoes, peeled and diced
1 garlic clove, minced
2 Tbsp (30 mL) salted butter
1 tsp (5 mL) truffle paste
2 Tbsp (30 mL) minced fresh chives or parsley
3 eggs, divided
Salt and pepper, to taste
1 cup (250 mL) Panko breadcrumbs
4 cups (1 L) grapeseed or vegetable oil, for frying

1. Place the potatoes in a saucepan and cover with cold water. Bring to a boil, then reduce heat to a simmer and cook until the potatoes are cooked and soft, about 10 minutes. Drain and mash the potatoes with a ricer or a potato masher. Add the garlic, butter, truffle paste, and herbs. Add 1 egg and stir to mix until smooth. Season well with salt and pepper and stir to mix. Refrigerate for 15 minutes. With a small scoop or spoon, take a small walnut-sized lump of dough. Form into a ball with your hands and repeat with remainder. Refrigerate the balls for at least 1 hour.
2. In a mixing bowl, whisk the last two eggs. Place the breadcrumbs on a plate. Dip the chilled potato balls in the egg mixture, and then roll in the breadcrumbs to coat. (Croquettes can be chilled until needed.)
3. In a large pot, heat the oil to 375°F (190°C). Add the croquettes in batches and fry until golden brown. Remove and place on a plate lined with paper towels. Serve warm with mushroom aïoli (p. 96).

MUSHROOM HUMMUS

SERVES 6–8

Hummus is one of my favourite things to slather on fresh bread. I also like to use it as a base for chunks of smoked salmon or tuna to make a great first course of a meal. Just place a dollop of the hummus on the plate, top with the smoked fish, add a few olives, a drizzle of olive oil, and a squeeze of lemon juice.

5 Tbsp (75 mL) olive oil, divided
2 cups (500 mL) chopped mushrooms
1 Tbsp (15 mL) chopped garlic
Salt and pepper, to taste
2 cups (500 mL) cooked chickpeas
Zest and juice of 1 lemon
1 tsp (5 mL) hot sauce

1. In a skillet over medium-high heat, add 1 tablespoon (15 mL) of the olive oil and the mushrooms. Stir until the mushrooms begin to wilt and soften slightly. Add the garlic, season with salt and pepper, and sauté until the mushrooms begin to brown. Remove from heat, set aside, and let cool slightly.
2. In a food processor, purée the mushrooms and chickpeas until a coarse mixture forms. Add the lemon zest and juice. Continue to purée the mixture, adding the remaining olive oil in a slow stream until the mixture is very smooth. Add the hot sauce and season well with salt and pepper. Pulse to mix, then transfer to a serving dish, drizzle with a little more olive oil, and serve with rustic bread, pita bread, or porcini naan (p. 144).

PICKLED MUSHROOMS

MAKES ABOUT 4 CUPS (1 L)

This is one of my favourite things to make during the fall mushroom season. I use chanterelles whenever possible and toss in assorted mushrooms like oysters, hedgehogs, cauliflower fungi, and boletes. The rest of the year, I use shiitakes, buttons, shimeji, and dried morels. Whatever the combination used, this dish is always a hit.

1 cup (250 mL) vinegar
½ cup (125 mL) honey
1 Tbsp (15 mL) pickling spice
1 medium onion, chopped
1 sweet red pepper, seeded and diced
2 cups (500 mL) sliced fresh or dried mushrooms

1. In a saucepan, bring the vinegar, honey, pickling spice, onion, pepper, and mushrooms to a boil. Reduce heat and simmer for 10 minutes. Remove from heat and let cool.
2. I usually use this recipe as a quick pickle and keep it in the refrigerator for up to one month. For home canning tips and rules, see bernardin.ca or freshpreserving.com.

CONSERVA OF PORCINI MUSHROOMS, CAPERS, AND LEMON

MAKES 4 CUPS (1 L)

This combination of fresh porcini, garlic, and lemon will transport you to the tapas bars of Spain. A great accompaniment to a tapas table, conserva is excellent with crusty bread or spooned over a piece of pan-roasted fish.

¼ cup (60 mL) olive oil, divided
1 cup (250 mL) finely diced onions
1 lb (450 g) porcini mushrooms (or buttons, chanterelles, etc.)
2 Tbsp (30 mL) minced garlic
1 cup (250 mL) stewed (and crushed) tomatoes
Zest and juice of 1 lemon
1 Tbsp (15 mL) small capers
2 Tbsp (30 mL) chopped fresh marjoram, thyme, or flat-leaf parsley
Salt and pepper, to taste

1. In a skillet, heat about 2 tablespoons (30 mL) of the oil and then add the onions. Sauté until the onions soften and begin to brown. Add the porcini and garlic and sauté until the mushrooms lose moisture and begin to brown. Add the tomatoes, lemon zest and juice, capers, and herbs. Cook, stirring constantly until the tomato reduces to a thick paste. Add the reserved olive oil and season well with salt and pepper. Let cool and serve at room temperature over grilled bread or oysters.

MUSHROOM CHUTNEY

MAKES ABOUT 8 CUPS (2 L)

This sweet and sour mix is a versatile blend that can be used in a number of applications. It's great on a cheese plate and excellent as a condiment in sandwiches. A great mushroom for this recipe is the chanterelle, but shiitakes, oysters, hedgehogs, and pine mushrooms are also good choices.

2 Tbsp (30 mL) mustard seeds
10 whole cloves
6 black peppercorns
1 cinnamon stick
1 bay leaf
1 tsp (5 mL) dry mustard powder
½ tsp (2 mL) ground turmeric
1 Tbsp (15 mL) minced fresh ginger
1 tsp (5 mL) salt
1 Tbsp (15 mL) vegetable oil
2 cups (500 mL) diced onions
4 cups (1 L) chopped mushrooms (chanterelle, shiitake, etc.)
1 Tbsp (15 mL) minced garlic
1 cup (250 mL) raisins
1 cup (250 mL) white vinegar
½ cup (125 mL) white sugar

1. In large saucepan, over medium heat, toast the mustard seeds, cloves, peppercorns, cinnamon stick, bay leaf, dry mustard, turmeric, ginger, and salt until mustard seeds begin to pop, about 1 minute. Remove from heat. Grind in a spice grinder or use a mortar and pestle.
2. Warm a heavy-bottomed saucepan over medium heat. Add the oil, onions, mushrooms, garlic, and raisins and cook until the onions begins to soften. Add the spice mix and cook, stirring often, for 5 minutes. Add the vinegar and sugar; bring to boil. Reduce the heat and simmer for 10 minutes. Remove from heat and let cool. Can be refrigerated for up to 1 month.

TOMATO AND PINE MUSHROOM COMPOTE

MAKES ABOUT 6 CUPS (1.5 L)

The combination of tomatoes and pine mushrooms is magical, much like the effect of basil with tomatoes. Chanterelles are also a good choice. This compote is great with steamed or grilled fish.

2 cups (500 mL) chopped tomatoes (fresh or canned)
1 cup (250 mL) diced onions
1 cup (250 mL) trimmed and diced celery
½ cup (125 mL) brown sugar
½ cup (125 mL) vinegar
1 Tbsp (15 mL) pickling spice
1 Tbsp (15 mL) minced fresh ginger
2 cups (500 mL) pine mushrooms

1. In a stockpot, combine the tomatoes, onions, celery, brown sugar, vinegar, pickling spice, ginger, and pine mushrooms. Bring to a boil, then reduce the heat and simmer for 15 minutes, or until the vegetables are soft.
2. Transfer to a glass jar and store in the fridge for up to 2 weeks.

MUSHROOM KETCHUP

MAKES ABOUT 6 CUPS (1.5 L)

A variation on a traditional English recipe that makes a delicious and versatile condiment. There are many recipes that require you to salt the mushrooms for 24 hours before using but I don't really see the need for this step. If you cook out the purée, blend it until smooth, and keep it in the fridge, this ketchup will be a great addition to your repertoire. If you use cultivated mushrooms, it will be easy to make year-round.

2 lb (1 kg) mushrooms (button, chanterelle, oyster, shiitake, etc.)
1 Tbsp (15 mL) porcini powder (p. 73)
1 medium onion, diced
1 medium celery stalk, trimmed and chopped
1 cup (250 mL) apple cider vinegar
½ cup (125 mL) brown sugar
1 tsp (5 mL) allspice
1 Tbsp (15 mL) minced fresh ginger
1 Tbsp (15 mL) minced garlic
¼ cup (60 mL) sweet sherry
Bay leaf
Hot sauce, to taste
Salt and pepper, to taste

1. In a heavy-bottomed saucepan, combine the mushrooms, porcini powder, onion, celery, vinegar, brown sugar, allspice, ginger, garlic, sherry, bay leaf, and hot sauce. Add 1 cup (250 mL) water and simmer over very low heat for about 1 hour. Stir constantly as the sugar will have a tendency to stick to the bottom of the pot. Add additional water if the mixture becomes too thick. Use a heat-reducing pad for your stove if you have issues.
2. Purée with an immersion blender or in a food processor. Taste and adjust seasoning with salt and pepper. It should be a nice blend of sweet and sour. Transfer to a glass mason jar, seal, and cool to room temperature. Store in the fridge for up to 2 months.

KOREAN-STYLE MUSHROOMS

MAKES 6–8 SERVINGS

A fresh style of kimchi designed to be mixed and eaten quickly. The spice level is low, so you can pump it up as much as you want. Great as a side dish with a variety of tapas or grilled beef.

1 lb (450 g) mushrooms (chanterelle, cauliflower fungus, hedgehog, button, etc.)
1 Tbsp (15 mL) grapeseed oil
2 Tbsp (30 mL) rice vinegar
1 Tbsp (15 mL) Japanese soy sauce
1 tsp (5 mL) shiro (light) miso paste (or Korean miso-chili paste)
1 tsp (5 mL) hot sauce
1 Tbsp (15 mL) minced garlic
1 tsp (5 mL) sesame oil
Salt and pepper, to taste

1. Clean mushrooms and rip into pieces. In a saucepan over medium-high heat, sauté mushrooms in grapeseed oil until liquid is released. Continue sautéing until liquid evaporates, then add the vinegar, soy sauce, miso, hot sauce, garlic, and sesame oil. Sauté until the seasonings are absorbed. Check the seasoning and adjust with salt and pepper. Transfer to a serving bowl and serve warm or chilled.

If you can find a Korean fermented bean paste called *gochujang* or its milder cousin *ssamjang*, use it in place of the miso for a more authentic result.

JAPANESE PICKLED MUSHROOMS

MAKES 6–8 SERVINGS

This Japanese-flavoured dish is excellent as a side to seafood and pork dishes. Adding this pickle to steamed rice would make a quick lunch or an elegant starter.

1 lb (450 g) mushrooms (button, oyster, shiitake, enoki, etc.)
1 cup (250 mL) rice wine vinegar
1 Tbsp (15 mL) Japanese soy sauce
1 Tbsp (15 mL) mirin (or honey)
1 tsp (5 mL) wasabi paste
1 Tbsp (15 mL) minced pickled ginger
1 tsp (5 mL) sesame oil

1. Place all ingredients in a non-stick skillet, bring to a boil, and remove from heat. Let stand for 15 minutes. Transfer to a storage container and refrigerate for at least 30 minutes. If you have any leftover sauce after eating the mushrooms, it makes a great addition to salad dressings.

MUSHROOM BORANI

SERVES 4

Borani is a dish with Persian roots that is essentially a mixture of vegetables and yogurt. This version is loaded with mushrooms and makes a light and healthy appetizer that is also perfect for light meals and gatherings.

2 Tbsp (30 mL) olive oil
1 onion, finely minced
2 cups (500 mL) sliced mushrooms (chanterelle, button, oyster, shiitake, etc.)
4 garlic cloves, finely minced
1 lb (450 g) fresh spinach, washed and trimmed
Salt and pepper, to taste
1 cup (250 mL) thick yogurt (Greek or Balkan style)
½ cup (125 mL) chopped fresh mint (or cilantro or parsley)

1. Warm a skillet over medium-high heat, then add the olive oil and onion. Brown the onion lightly and then add the mushrooms and garlic. Toss well to mix and sauté until the mushrooms release moisture and the pan becomes dry again. Add the spinach, tossing to wilt it. Season the mixture with salt and pepper. Transfer to a bowl and let cool completely. Refrigerate until chilled.
2. Once mixture is cooled, add the yogurt and fresh mint. Adjust the seasoning with salt and pepper. Serve with fresh pita bread or naan.

JAPANESE-STYLE ENOKI MUSHROOMS AND SPINACH GOMA-AE

SERVES 4

Goma means "sesame" in Japanese and refers to the seasoning on this rice and mushroom dish. You can also use kale or stinging nettles with excellent results. Make sure to squeeze as much moisture as possible from the spinach before adding the seasonings. Too much moisture will dilute the impact of the dressing. Add the enoki mushrooms at the last minute to preserve the crunch of the mushrooms.

1 lb (450 g) spinach
2 Tbsp (30 mL) shiro (light) miso paste
1 Tbsp (15 mL) grapeseed oil
1 tsp (5 mL) sesame oil
1 Tbsp (15 mL) mirin
1 Tbsp (15 mL) white sesame seeds
3.5 oz (100 g) enoki mushrooms

1. In a large pot of boiling salted water, add the spinach and boil for 1 minute. Drain. Squeeze excess water from the spinach; set aside until needed.
2. In a mixing bowl, combine the miso, grapeseed oil, sesame oil, and mirin. Whisk until uniform, then add the spinach and sesame seeds and toss well to mix. Let stand for 5 minutes to infuse. Before serving, chop the enoki mushrooms into small pieces. Mix into the spinach and serve at room temperature.

SAUTÉED CHANTERELLES, CABBAGE, AND BACON

SERVES 4

The classic combination of bacon and cabbage soars with the added punch of chanterelle mushrooms. Many other mushrooms work well in this recipe, including button mushrooms, shiitakes, oysters, hedgehogs, shimeji, and cauliflower fungi.

2 strips bacon
1 onion, thinly sliced
2 cups (500 mL) cleaned and sliced chanterelle mushrooms
1 Tbsp (15 mL) minced garlic
2 cups (500 mL) thinly sliced cabbage
Salt and pepper, to taste

1. Warm a sauté pan over medium-high heat, then add the bacon and cook until it starts to crisp. Add the onion and chanterelles and sauté until soft and beginning to brown. Add the garlic and cabbage. Season with salt and pepper. Cook until the cabbage just begins to wilt.

PÂTÉS AND CHARCUTERIE

MUSHROOM PÂTÉ

SERVIES 4

This pâté works with a wide variety of mushrooms. Mixed wild mushrooms or cultivated mushrooms are equally good. My favourites are oyster mushrooms, chanterelles, and shiitakes. They have a strong flavour that balances nicely with the cream or goat cheese.

---

1 Tbsp (15 mL) salted butter
1 small onion, finely minced
2 Tbsp (30 mL) minced garlic
2 cups (500 mL) diced assorted mushrooms
1 cup (250 mL) cream cheese or goat cheese
2 Tbsp (30 mL) chopped fresh herbs (parsley, sage, marjoram, etc.)
1 tsp (5 mL) ground pepper
1 tsp (5 mL) lemon zest
1 tsp (5 mL) lemon juice

---

1. In a skillet over medium-high heat, warm the butter until sizzling, then add the onion, garlic, and mushrooms. Sauté until the mushrooms release their liquid and begin to brown. Remove from heat and let cool. Add the cheese, herbs, pepper, lemon zest, and lemon juice. With a spatula or spoon, mash the cheese until finely blended. Place in a serving container and chill until needed. Can also be rolled into a log, covered with plastic wrap, and chilled. Just before serving, the log can be cut into rounds for a nice presentation.

CHICKEN LIVER AND MUSHROOM PÂTÉ

SERVES 4–6

The secret to this pâté is to not overcook the liver. Liver gets grainy and strongly flavoured when cooked too long. Keep the centres pink and the result should be delicious. I like preparing this pâté with button mushrooms. They add lightness and smoothness to the mix but still highlight the flavour of the liver purée. This dish is also excellent made with duck livers.

½ lb (225 g) chicken livers
3 Tbsp (45 mL) sweet sherry, divided
Salt and pepper, to taste
1 Tbsp (15 mL) salted butter
1 cup (250 mL) chopped button mushrooms
1 shallot, diced
1 garlic clove, chopped
1 Tbsp (15 mL) chopped fresh thyme
¼ cup (60 mL) salted butter, cut into cubes

1. Place the chicken livers in a bowl and rinse with cold water. Remove as much blood as possible. Try to remove any veins or pieces of liver that are stained green. Drain and add 2 tablespoons (30 mL) of the sherry to the livers. Season with salt and pepper and let stand for at least 15 minutes.
2. In a skillet, heat the butter over medium-high heat. When it is sizzling, add the livers, mushrooms, shallot, garlic, and thyme. Cook for 1–2 minutes per side or until the livers are browned but still rare in the centre. Add remaining sherry and deglaze the pan. Transfer everything to the bowl of a food processor, scraping all the bits off the bottom of the pan. While still warm, process the livers until smooth, adding the cubes of butter until they have all been incorporated. Season well with more salt and pepper. Transfer to a serving bowl, cool to room temperature, and place in the fridge to chill for at least 1 hour. Serve with fresh baguette.

DUCK AND MUSHROOM RILLETTES

SERVES 4

A spin on the classic French appetizer, this recipe can be made with many confit items, including pork shoulder and rabbit. If you want to keep the rillettes for an extended time, you should cover the finished product with a layer of liquid duck fat. Once it chills, it will keep for about one week in the fridge or one month in the freezer.

2 duck leg confit (p. 132)
4 Tbsp (60 mL) duck fat
2 cups (500 mL) mushrooms (chanterelle, button, porcini, etc.)
Salt and pepper, to taste

1. Pick apart the duck and remove any bones, as well as the hard leg tendons. In a skillet over medium-high heat, add half the duck fat and the mushrooms. Sauté until the mushrooms give off moisture and all the moisture is evaporated. Let the mushrooms just begin to brown.
2. Add the mushrooms to a food processor along with the remaining duck meat and duck fat. Pulse gently to combine, retaining a little texture. Taste and season the mixture. Pour into a glass jar and cool slightly. Place the jar in the fridge and cool completely, about 2 hours. To serve, spread on fresh baguette.

COUNTRY-STYLE PÂTÉ WITH MORELS AND LEEKS

MAKES 10 SERVINGS

A coarse country pâté that is more like meatloaf than smooth liver-based pâtés. Great served with Dijon mustard, pickles, and fresh baguette. This version is made without commercial preservatives (nitrates), so it should be used within a few days or frozen for up to a month.

½ cup (125 mL) dried morels
1 cup (250 mL) boiling water
1 Tbsp (15 mL) butter or olive oil
1 cup (250 mL) chopped and washed leeks
1 Tbsp (15 mL) minced garlic
3 Tbsp (45 mL) minced fresh herbs (parsley, sage, thyme, rosemary, etc.)
Salt and pepper, to taste
1 lb (450 g) bacon
2 lb (1 kg) ground pork
1 egg
1 Tbsp (15 mL) salt
1 tsp (5 mL) ground black pepper

1. In a small metal bowl, add the morels to the boiling water and set aside for 1 hour. Meanwhile, heat a skillet over medium-high. Add the butter (or olive oil) and then the leeks to the pan. Sauté until the leeks soften and begin to brown. Add the garlic and herbs and season well with salt and pepper. Cook until all the moisture is evaporated and the pan is dry. Set aside and let cool completely.
2. Preheat the oven to 325°F (160°C).
3. Take half the bacon and mince to a coarse consistency (or pulse in a food processor for a finer consistency). Line a terrine mould (or bread tin) with the remaining rashers of bacon. In a mixing bowl, combine the ground pork, minced bacon, egg, leek mixture, salt, and pepper. Drain the morels, then chop into coarse pieces and add to the mix. With washed hands, mix until a smooth consistency is reached, 1–2 minutes. Cook a small patty in a skillet to taste the seasoning. Adjust with salt and pepper.
4. With wet hands, place the mixture in the terrine (or loaf tin) and pat down to remove any air bubbles. Cover with a rectangle of aluminum foil, fitting it into the edges of the container. Top with the terrine lid or a double layer of foil. Boil a kettle of water and half fill a shallow casserole into which the terrine pan will fit. Place in the oven and add the terrine to the water bath. Cook for 1½–2 hours, or until the internal temperature reaches 150°F (65°C), or a knife inserted into the terrine is hot and the juices run clear.
5. Remove from the oven, let cool, and place a weight (a brick covered in aluminum foil works well) on top to compress the terrine. Place in the fridge and chill completely before serving.

BEEF, CHANTERELLE, AND CHEESE CURD TERRINE

MAKES 8 PORTIONS

This recipe uses cheese curd and mushrooms to add texture and flavour to the terrine. The loaf can be served warm or cold. The texture improves if the loaf is chilled before serving. You can reheat the whole loaf or reheat slices in the oven or a skillet. It makes a great sandwich as well. It is obviously important that the chanterelles be very clean and free of all dirt and sand before being added to the terrine. This recipe also works with many other types of mushrooms, including cultivated types.

Terrine
2 lb (1 kg) ground beef
½ lb (225 g) fresh cheese curd
2 cups (500 mL) cleaned and diced chanterelle mushrooms
1 Tbsp (15 mL) chopped fresh rosemary
1 Tbsp (15 mL) chopped fresh sage
1 Tbsp (15 mL) sea salt
1 tsp (5 mL) fresh ground black pepper
1 Tbsp (15 mL) minced garlic
1 egg

Horseradish cream
1 cup (250 mL) sour cream
2 Tbsp (30 mL) grated fresh horseradish (or to taste)
Salt and pepper, to taste

1. Preheat the oven to 350°F (180°C).
2. In a mixing bowl, combine the beef, cheese curd, mushrooms, rosemary, sage, salt, pepper, garlic, and egg. Mix well with clean hands until a smooth consistency is reached.
3. Pack the meat mixture into a loaf tin. Press with your fingers to remove any pockets of air. Transfer the loaf tin to a baking tray and place in the oven for 30 minutes, or until a knife inserted in the middle comes out hot—the temperature should be greater than 300°F (150°C) and the juices should run clear. Remove from the oven and let cool. When the terrine has reached room temperature, cover with plastic wrap and place in the fridge until set, at least 2 hours.
4. In a small bowl, combine the sour cream and horseradish. Season with salt and pepper, then cover with plastic wrap and chill until needed.
5. To serve, unwrap the chilled terrine and cut into thick slices. Place sliced loaf onto a baking tray and reheat for 10 minutes in a 350°F (180°C) oven.

PORK AND MUSHROOM SAUSAGE WITH ASIAN FLAVOURS

MAKES ABOUT 16 SAUSAGES

This method is for sausages, but you can also form patties and skip the stuffing process. I use the grinder and sausage attachments of my KitchenAid stand mixer with good results. Start with a pork shoulder if you go this route and use local artisan pork for the best results. The mushrooms add moisture and texture to the sausage.

4 lb (2 kg) ground pork
1 cup (250 mL) water
2 Tbsp (30 mL) sea salt
1 Tbsp (15 mL) hot sauce
1 Tbsp (15 mL) minced garlic
1 Tbsp (15 mL) minced fresh ginger
2 Tbsp (30 mL) soy sauce
4 cups (1 L) chopped mushrooms (button, shiitake, chanterelle, etc.)
4 Tbsp (60 mL) minced fresh cilantro
Sausage casing (natural or cellulose, available from butchers and butcher supply shops)

1. Chill the pork until very cold (place in the freezer for 15 minutes). In a bowl, mix the water, salt, hot sauce, garlic, ginger, and soy sauce. Stir well to mix and dissolve the salt. Add the meat, mushrooms, and cilantro and work in the seasoning with clean hands. Knead until all the liquid is absorbed and the meat texture looks consistent and is beginning to get sticky, which is important for developing the correct texture of a well-made sausage. Test the seasoning by placing a spoonful in a skillet and cooking completely. Adjust seasonings to taste. Cover with plastic wrap and chill for at least 30 minutes.
2. Using a sausage stuffer (or mixer attachment), place the sausage casing onto the end of the stuffer tube. If cranking by hand, use a slow and steady rotation until you get a handle on the speed of the stuffer. If using a grinder with a sausage stuffer attachment, you will need two people: one person adds the filling to the stuffer while the other guides the sausage out.
3. Watching as the sausage meat exits the end of the stuffer tube, fill the sausage casing until it is full (check for air bubbles). You will be able to feel with your fingers when the sausage is firm, not too loose (air bubbles) nor too tight. A loose filling makes for an unattractive sausage but you can fix this problem by squeezing the filling into a firm mass when you make 6-inch (15 cm) sausage links. Too much filling will cause the casing to burst; if this happens, you will have to stop and return the filling to the hopper (so avoid doing this too often).
4. Coil the sausage into a clean pan or tray while making one large continuous link. Make individual sausages by twisting the sausage at 6-inch (15 cm) intervals. For best results, cut the sausage into links and freeze on a tray. Once frozen, remove from the tray and wrap in waxed butcher paper. Use within 2 months for best results.

WÜSTHOF

MUSHROOM DUCK CONFIT

MAKES 4 PIECES

Duck confit is one of my favourite things. When I hit upon the idea of using mushroom powder, it was easily the best confit I've ever made. The mushroom powder makes the skin very crispy and incredibly delicious. You can boost the mushroom content further by sprinkling fresh mushroom powder on the duck confit just before you reheat it. Save the fat as it makes excellent roasted potatoes or Yorkshire pudding (p. 100).

4 duck legs and thighs
1 Tbsp (15 mL) mushroom powder (porcini, shiitake, button, etc.) (p. 73)
4 garlic cloves, chopped
1 Tbsp (15 mL) chopped fresh thyme
1 Tbsp (15 mL) chopped fresh rosemary
1 Tbsp (15 mL) chopped fresh sage
4 Tbsp (60 mL) sea salt
1 Tbsp (15 mL) whole peppercorns
2 cups (500 mL) duck fat (or olive oil)

1. Trim the excess fat from the duck legs and thighs. Rub the skin with the mushroom powder and place in a glass or non-reactive dish. Add garlic, thyme, rosemary, sage, sea salt, and peppercorns. Toss well to mix and cover with plastic wrap. Refrigerate overnight, or for at least six hours.
2. Remove from juice and place in a clean roasting pan. Discard any liquid that is left but add any loose herbs. Cover the duck pieces with duck fat. Cover the pan with a lid or tinfoil to make a tight seal. Place in a 300°F (150°C) oven for 2 hours, or until the flesh is soft and easily comes off the bone. Confit is best chilled overnight in the fat. Remove from the fat and sear the outside in a non-stick skillet.

BREAD, FLATBREADS, AND SAVOURY CAKES

MAITAKE

PIZZA DOUGH

MAKES 2 SMALL PIZZAS OR 1 LARGE PIZZA

You can make your own pizza dough or go to your favourite bakery and ask them for some fresh dough balls (white or multi-grain).

1 cup (250 mL) beer (preferably lager or ale)
1 Tbsp (15 mL) white sugar
1¼ tsp (6.5 mL) dry instant yeast
1 tsp (5 mL) salt
1 Tbsp (15 mL) olive oil
2¾ cups (680 mL) bread flour
¼ cup (60 mL) semolina flour

1. Place beer in a measuring cup and heat to 100°F (38°C) in a water bath or microwave. Add the sugar and yeast to the beer. Let stand for 10 minutes to activate the yeast. Add this mixture to the bowl of a mixer with a dough hook (or use the dough cycle of a bread machine or mix and knead it by hand). Add the salt, olive oil, bread flour, and semolina. Work the dough until very smooth and elastic, about 10 minutes. Remove from the machine, place in an oiled bowl, and cover with plastic wrap. Cover with a clean kitchen towel and place in the fridge overnight to proof. The next day, punch down the dough and then use it in your favourite recipe.

MUSHROOM AND CHORIZO FLATBREAD

MAKES 1 LARGE RECTANGULAR FLATBREAD

This bread is excellent baked in the oven or barbecued on the grill using a pizza stone.

1 Tbsp (15 mL) olive oil
1 cup (250 mL) sliced onions
Salt and pepper, to taste
½ cup (125 mL) dry white wine or apple cider
2 cups (500 mL) sliced mushrooms (chanterelle, pine, button, porcini, etc.)
1 cup (250 mL) diced or crumbled chorizo
1 Tbsp (15 mL) minced garlic
1 tsp (5 mL) minced fresh sage
1 recipe pizza dough (p. 136)
Olive oil
Coarse sea salt

1. Preheat the oven to 400°F (200°C).
2. In a saucepan over medium-high heat, warm the olive oil and onions, seasoning with salt and pepper. Sauté until the onions begin to brown. Add the wine or cider and cook until all the liquid is reduced. Add the mushrooms and chorizo and sauté until the mushrooms soften and begin to brown. Add the garlic and sage. Season well with salt and pepper. Remove from heat and let cool.
3. Roll the dough into a large rectangle, about the size of a small baking sheet. Place dough on a greased baking sheet and let stand for 10 minutes. Sprinkle with olive oil and a light dusting of sea salt. Cover the surface with the cooled mushroom and chorizo mixture. Place flatbread in the oven and cook for 15–20 minutes, or until dough has risen and browned. Cut into thick squares and serve hot.

TARTE FLAMBÉ WITH MOREL MUSHROOMS AND BACON

MAKES 1 LARGE RECTANGULAR TARTE

I first tasted tarte flambé while working in Alsace, France. It was made with fresh porcini (called cèpe locally) and it made a huge impression on me. Use a rough ceramic pizza stone in your oven for best results. I have also made this dish on the barbecue with good results. Place the raw dough directly on the grill. When it has browned and stiffened up, flip the crust over and add toppings to the cooked side. Close the lid and finish cooking for 4–5 minutes.

¼ lb (about 115 g) slab bacon (or pork belly), cut into small cubes or thick slices
1 onion, sliced (or a washed and cleaned leek)
¼ cup (60 mL) dried morel mushrooms, soaked in water for 1 hour and then drained
¼ cup (60 mL) dry white wine
1 recipe pizza dough (p. 136)
1 cup (250 mL) sour cream
Salt and pepper, to taste

1. Preheat the oven to 425°F (220°C).
2. In a skillet over medium heat, add the bacon and onion. When the mixture has just begun to colour, add the morels and wine. Cook until the mixture has reduced down and the pan appears dry. Season with salt and pepper.
3. Cut dough into 2 equal portions and dust lightly with flour. Roll into a rectangle with an even thickness of about half an inch (about 1 cm) and place on an oiled baking tray. Spread half of the sour cream over the surface of the dough. Top with half of the bacon and half of the sliced onions. Season with salt and pepper. Repeat with remaining dough and ingredients.
4. Bake in the oven for 10–12 minutes, or until the crust is golden and crispy.

SEMOLINA MUSHROOM CAKE

SERVES 8–10

This cake is great as a side bread or can be used with any mushroom sauce to make a complete meal. A variety of vegetables can be added to the basic batter mix. You can use any firm mushrooms, such as buttons, chanterelles, or shiitakes. Leftovers are great pan-fried alongside eggs for breakfast.

1 cup (250 mL) semolina flour (or Cream of Wheat)
1 cup (250 mL) plain yogurt (Greek or Balkan style)
⅓ cup (85 mL) water (just enough to make a thick batter)
1 tsp (5 mL) yellow ground turmeric
1 tsp (5 mL) cumin powder
1 tsp (5 mL) baking soda
1 tsp (5 mL) salt
2 Tbsp (30 mL) grapeseed oil
1 Tbsp (15 mL) mustard seeds
1 Tbsp (15 mL) cumin seeds
1 Tbsp (15 mL) fennel seeds
1 small onion, finely chopped
2 cups (500 mL) finely chopped assorted mushrooms
1 green or red hot chili, finely chopped (or 1 Tbsp [15 mL] hot sauce)
¼ cup (60 mL) chopped cilantro
1 tsp (5 mL) grated fresh ginger
1 Tbsp (15 mL) minced or grated garlic
1 cup (250 mL) frozen peas
2 Tbsp (30 mL) sesame seeds

1. Preheat the oven to 350°F (180°C) and have all your ingredients ready before you start to mix the ingredients.
2. In a mixing bowl, combine the semolina and yogurt, mixing to make a paste. Add the water and stir until smooth. Add the turmeric, cumin powder, baking soda, and salt.
3. Immediately begin heating a skillet containing the oil. Once the pan is hot, add the mustard, cumin, and fennel seeds. Heat until you hear the seeds pop, about 1–2 minutes. Add the onion, mushrooms, and chili and toss well to coat. Sauté for 3–4 minutes then pour the mixture into the batter and stir quickly. Add the cilantro, ginger, garlic, and peas. Stir to mix.
4. Pour batter into an oiled casserole dish, smooth the top and sprinkle with the sesame seeds. Place in the oven and bake for about 25–30 minutes, or until the batter is set and the top is beginning to brown.

MUSHROOM VEGETABLE CORNBREAD

SERVES 6–8

This cornbread is a nice accompaniment to an outdoor barbecue or to serve alongside a heartier chowder. Use firm mushrooms, like buttons, shiitakes, or chanterelles for best results.

2 carrots, diced
1 onion, diced
1 cup (250 mL) trimmed and diced broccoli
1 cup (250 mL) corn kernels (fresh or frozen)
2 cups (500 mL) diced mushrooms
2 Tbsp (30 mL) olive oil
Salt and pepper, to taste
1½ cups (375 mL) medium-grind cornmeal
½ cup (125 mL) all-purpose flour
1½ tsp (7.5 mL) baking powder
1 tsp (5 mL) salt
1 Tbsp (15 mL) sugar
1 egg
1¼ cup (310 mL) buttermilk
1 Tbsp (15 mL) minced fresh rosemary
1 Tbsp (15 mL) minced fresh sage
1 Tbsp (15 mL) minced fresh garlic
2 Tbsp (30 mL) olive oil

1. Preheat the oven to 375°F (190°C).
2. On a baking tray, combine the carrots, onion, broccoli, corn, and mushrooms. Drizzle with olive oil and season with salt and pepper. Place in the oven and roast for 30 minutes or until the vegetables are soft and beginning to brown. Remove from the oven and let cool.
3. In a mixing bowl, combine the cornmeal, flour, baking powder, salt, and sugar. Mix the egg into the buttermilk and pour into the dry ingredients. If the mixture seems dry, add a few more splashes of buttermilk until a nice pourable batter is obtained. Fold in the rosemary, sage, garlic, and the roasted vegetables and any juices.
4. Place oil in a casserole dish and distribute it around the pan, then pour the batter overtop and smooth with a spatula or spoon. Place in the oven and bake for 30 minutes or until the top is nicely browned and the cake pulls away from the sides of the pan.

PORCINI NAAN

MAKES 6–8 LARGE NAAN

Naan is an Indian flatbread that is usually made in a tandoor oven. You can use a barbecue or an oven with a pizza baking stone with good results. Naan is great fresh off the grill and as a side for curries or grilled meats. Try this naan as a fresh wrap for grilled sausages topped with mushroom chutney (p. 112).

1 package instant dry yeast
1 cup (250 mL) warm water
¼ cup (60 mL) white sugar
3 Tbsp (45 mL) milk
1 egg, beaten
2 tsp (10 mL) salt
2 Tbsp (30 mL) porcini powder (p. 73)
4½ cups (1.125 L) bread flour
1 Tbsp (15 mL) minced garlic
¼ cup (60 mL) melted butter

1. In a large bowl, dissolve yeast in warm water. Let stand for about 10 minutes, until frothy. Stir in sugar, milk, egg, salt, porcini powder, and enough flour to make a soft dough. Knead for 6–8 minutes on a lightly floured surface, or until smooth. Place dough in a well-oiled bowl, cover with a damp cloth, and set aside to rise. Let it rise 1 hour, until the dough has doubled in size.
2. Punch down the dough and knead in the garlic. Pinch off small handfuls of dough about the size of a golf ball. Roll into balls, and place on a tray. Cover with a towel, and let rise until doubled in size, about 30 minutes. Roll out the dough into 6–8 thin circles. Preheat the grill to high heat.
3. Lightly oil the grill. Place dough rounds on the grill, in batches, and cook for 2–3 minutes, or until puffy and lightly browned. Brush uncooked side with butter, and turn over. Brush cooked side with butter, and cook until the underside is browned and the naan puffs up, about 2–3 minutes. Remove from the grill, and repeat the process until all the naan have been prepared.

GREEN ONION AND MUSHROOM PANCAKES

MAKES ABOUT 16 PANCAKES

These addictive rounds are wonderful on their own or as the foundation for an appetizer with smoked salmon or sautéed mushrooms. Uncooked rounds freeze nicely and can be cooked from their frozen state at a later date. Keeps frozen for up to one month.

3 cups (750 mL) bread flour
1¼ cup (310 mL) boiling water
Vegetable oil, for brushing
1 tsp (5 mL) salt
Pepper, to taste
4 fresh shiitake mushrooms, minced
4 green onions, minced
2 Tbsp (30 mL) vegetable oil, for frying

1. In a food processor, add the flour and pour the boiling water overtop. Process until the mixture comes together in a ball (add more water if necessary). Dump the mixture onto a countertop and knead the dough until smooth. The dough will be quite firm. Place in a bowl and cover with plastic wrap. Let rest at room temperature for 1 hour.
2. Divide the dough into 16 equal pieces and shape them into rounds. Using a rolling pin, roll each one into a thin circle about 6 inches (15 cm) across. Brush lightly with vegetable oil and season well with salt and pepper. Sprinkle mushrooms and green onions overtop half of each surface. Roll up like a cigar and pinch the ends to seal. Take the cigar and coil the dough into a circle (like you are making a cinnamon bun). Pat down with your hand to make a flat, round disc. Liberally dust a work area with flour and roll out the disc until approximately 4 inches (10 cm) wide, dusting with more flour if needed. Repeat with remaining discs.
3. Warm a skillet over medium heat, then add 2 tablespoons (30 mL) vegetable oil. Fry the discs in batches until golden brown, about 2–3 minutes per side. Place the fried pancakes on a paper-towel-lined tray; place the tray in a 200°F (95°C) oven to keep pancakes warm. Continue with the rest of the dough.

MUSHROOM CROQUE MONSIEUR

SERVES 4

This recipe works great with leftover béchamel. If you make the full recipe, use any leftovers to make an excellent porcini macaroni and cheese (p. 167). Works well with any sharp cheese like aged cheddar, Gouda, or Manchego (Spanish sheep cheese).

1 tsp (5 mL) salted butter
1 cup (250 mL) sliced button mushrooms
Salt and pepper, to taste
1 cup (250 mL) porcini béchamel sauce (p. 224)
½ cup (125 mL) shredded Gruyère cheese
8 slices crusty French bread
4 slices ham (optional)
1 Tbsp (15 mL) butter, for frying

1. In a skillet over medium-high heat, add the butter and mushrooms and sauté until the mushrooms soften and begin to brown. Season with salt and pepper and set aside.
2. Place the béchamel in a saucepan and reheat over medium-low. If the mixture is thick, you can thin it with a little additional milk. When mixture is hot, stir in the cheese, remove from heat, and stir to melt. Adjust the seasoning with salt and pepper, to taste. Lay 4 slices of bread on a cutting board and spread with half the béchamel sauce. Top each slice with a quarter of the sautéed mushrooms and a slice of ham, if using. Top with a second slice of bread and finish this slice with a smear of béchamel.
3. Warm a non-stick skillet over medium heat, add 1 tablespoon (15 mL) butter and swirl to coat the bottom of the pan. Place the sandwiches cheese side down in the pan and top with the remaining béchamel. Cook for 2–3 minutes. Gently flip over the sandwiches and cook the other side until golden brown. The cheese sauce should make a solid crust if you don't move the sandwiches around too much while you are cooking them. (If you have a panini grill, you can also use it for this recipe.) Serve hot with a side of sweet and sour pickles.

APPETIZERS AND STARTER PLATES

DRIED PORCINI MUSHROOMS

BEEF TENDERLOIN AND OYSTER MUSHROOM CARPACCIO WITH CAESAR DRESSING

SERVES 4

An elegant dish that should only be made with very fresh beef from a source you trust. I use grass-fed beef and make sure it is in prime condition. If you like, you can cook the tenderloin to medium rare and let stand until cool. It will be similar but not quite as impactful as this blue rare version.

Tenderloin

1 lb (450 g) beef tenderloin
1 Tbsp (15 mL) mushroom powder (porcini or shiitake) (p. 73)
Salt and pepper, to taste
1 Tbsp (15 mL) salted butter
1 Tbsp (15 mL) olive oil
½ lb (225 g) oyster mushrooms

Dressing

1 garlic clove, finely minced
1 tsp (5 mL) minced anchovy (or anchovy paste)
1 tsp (5 mL) Worcestershire sauce
1 Tbsp (15 mL) yellow mustard
1 tsp (5 mL) hot sauce
1 Tbsp (15 mL) mayonnaise
1 Tbsp (15 mL) olive oil
¼ cup (60 mL) grated Parmesan cheese

1. Trim tenderloin of any sinew or fat. Season with mushroom powder, salt, and pepper. Warm a skillet over medium-high heat. Add the butter and oil, then sear the tenderloin until well browned but still completely raw inside, about 1–2 minutes per side. Transfer to a plate and cool to room temperature. Chill in the fridge for 1 hour.
2. When beef is chilled, wrap in plastic wrap and form into a tight log by twisting the ends of the plastic to form a sausage shape. Place the beef in the freezer until partially frozen. Remove the plastic wrap. Cut into thin slices with a very sharp knife (or a meat slicer). Place on serving plates, fanning several slices on one side of the plate. (The beef can be made in advance: sprinkle with a little olive oil, cover with plastic wrap, and chill.)
3. To prepare the dressing, combine the garlic and anchovy in a mixing bowl. With a spoon, smash them together into a paste. Add the Worcestershire sauce, mustard, hot sauce, and 1 tablespoon (15 mL) water. Whisk to mix, then add the mayonnaise and olive oil and stir well to blend. Add the grated cheese and keep chilled until needed. Before serving, warm a skillet over medium-high heat. Add 1 tablespoon (15 mL) olive oil and the oyster mushrooms and sauté until the mushrooms soften. Set aside.
4. To serve, unwrap the tenderloin plates. Mound the oyster mushrooms in the centre and drizzle with a little of the Caesar dressing. Season with salt and pepper and squeeze with a little lemon. Serve with good crusty bread.

ROASTED TOMATO STUFFED WITH PORCINI AND MOZZARELLA

SERVES 4

This dish is made for the fall when you have a ripe heirloom tomato and the first porcini of the year. You can also use 1 ounce (28 g) of dried porcini that have been rehydrated in water. This recipe also works well with chanterelles, hedgehogs, cauliflowers, and pine mushrooms. I use a fresh soft mozzarella—buffalo when I can get it—that you will find in the stores labelled as bocconcini or burrata.

4 medium tomatoes
1 recipe garlic confit (see sidebar)
½ cup (125 mL) cubed porcini mushrooms
4 fresh sage leaves, minced
Salt and pepper, to taste
1 cup (250 mL) fresh mozzarella cheese
1 Tbsp (15 mL) good balsamic vinegar
4 slices prosciutto, for garnish (optional)

1. Preheat the oven to 350°F (180°C).
2. Cut the top off each tomato and remove the seeds and interior with a spoon. Place the tomatoes on a roasting pan. In a skillet over medium-high heat, add a little of the garlic confit oil and sauté the porcini until lightly browned. Stuff each tomato with the garlic confit, sautéed porcini, and sage leaves. Season with salt and pepper and top with cubed or torn mozzarella.
3. Place stuffed tomatoes in the oven and bake for 15 mintues, or until cheese has melted and is beginning to brown. (You can turn on the broiler near the end to give it a nice crust.) To serve, transfer to a serving plate, drizzle with balsamic vinegar, and top with a crumbled slice of fresh prosciutto. Serve with good bread to mop up all the juices.

GARLIC CONFIT

1 bulb garlic, peeled into cloves
¼ cup (60 mL) olive oil

Place peeled garlic cloves in a small skillet. Cover with olive oil. Bring to a simmer, then transfer to a warm oven and cook for 15 minutes, or until soft and golden brown. Remove from the oven and let cool. Use the garlic to flavour dishes or as a spread over bread. Use the oil as a flavouring for cooking or salads. You can brush fresh bread with the oil and grill it for a delicious bruschetta.

WILD MUSHROOM, LEEK, AND BACON TARTE

MAKES 8 SERVINGS

This tarte takes me back to my time in France. In Alsace, the preferred mushroom would be the parasol mushroom but it is also very good with morels, porcini, oyster mushrooms, and even truffle paste. The tarte can be made in advance and kept for several days in the fridge. It would make a great lunch or dinner served with a lightly dressed salad of mixed greens.

2 medium leeks, trimmed and washed
6 slices bacon, cut into thin strips (crosswise)
4 cups (1 L) sliced mushrooms (button, chanterelle, pine, cauliflower, etc.)
¼ cup (60 mL) dry white wine or apple cider
1 recipe basic flaky pie dough, chilled (p. 97)
2 cups (500 mL) whipping cream or Creamo (half-and-half)
4 eggs
1 tsp (5 mL) trimmed and chopped fresh thyme
Salt and pepper, to taste

1. Cut the leeks into thin strips, using the white and light green parts only. Warm a skillet over medium-high heat. Add the bacon and cook until it begins to brown and renders fat, then pour off most of the fat and discard it. Add the leeks and mushrooms, stirring until they begin to soften and brown. Add the wine or cider and cook until the mixture is completely evaporated. Season well with salt and pepper, then let cool to room temperature.
2. Roll out the chilled, rested dough onto a well-floured surface. Place the dough into a pie tin, preferably one with a removable metal bottom and a fluted edge. Keep the dough very slack around the edge of the pie tin. Chill the dough for at least 15 minutes while you preheat the oven to 350°F (180°C). After removing the dough from the fridge, place a sheet of aluminum foil in the tin and roll the edges so the foil sheet fits snugly in the tin. Bake in the oven for 15 minutes, removing the foil for the last 5 minutes of cooking.
3. Meanwhile in a mixing bowl, add the mushroom and leek mixture. Pour in the cream and add the eggs. Whisk until mixed. Add the thyme and season well with salt and pepper. Pour the mixture into the hot pie shell, place on a tray and return to the oven. Reduce the heat to 325°F (160°C) and cook for 40 minutes, or until the tart filling is browned and starts to puff slightly. Remove from the oven and place on a cooling rack. Serve warm, or chill and reheat before serving.

CRAB AND PINE MUSHROOM CAKES

MAKES 8 CAKES

These crab cakes are moist and full of crab and mushroom flavour. Enoki mushrooms also work well with this dish for a milder mushroom flavour. The cakes can be made several hours in advance and heated to order. These cakes go great with mushroom aïoli (p. 96).

1 lb (450 g) white fish (cod, halibut, sole)
¼ cup (60 mL) whipping cream
2 cups (500 mL) crabmeat (from a 1½ lb [680 g] crab)
1 cup (250 mL) finely diced pine mushrooms
1 tsp (5 mL) minced garlic
1 green onion, thinly sliced
Salt and pepper, to taste
1 cup (250 mL) Panko or breadcrumbs
2 Tbsp (30 mL) canola oil

1. In a food processor, pulse the fish until a rough paste is formed. Add the cream and process until a smooth paste is obtained. Transfer to a mixing bowl and add the crab (without any juice), pine mushrooms, garlic, green onion, salt, and pepper. Mix until a smooth mixture is formed. The mixture should form into a ball without too much effort. If it is too wet, you can add a few breadcrumbs until a drier mixture is formed. Cook a small sample to test for seasoning and adjust if needed.
2. Using an ice cream scoop (or ¼ cup [60 mL] measure), take a scoop of the mixture and form it into a ball with your hands. Place in the Panko or breadcrumbs and roll to coat evenly. Press the ball to form a cake and place on a tray lined with parchment (or silicon) paper. Repeat with remaining crab mixture.
3. Heat a non-stick skillet with the oil, add the crab cakes (in batches if needed), and fry until golden brown on each side. Transfer to a warm oven and let rest while you finish cooking the remaining cakes. Serve warm with coleslaw or mayonnaise flavoured with lemon and garlic.

BRAISED MORELS STUFFED WITH CHORIZO AND OLIVES

SERVES 4

I use extra-large morels graded for their huge size. If you have smaller morels, around the size of your thumb, use two or three mushrooms per serving. Soak the morels in hot water for at least 20 minutes. They should swell up and be pliable when they are ready to use. The morels will be cooked again in wine or cider (or vegetable stock). You can skip the dressing and just finish the cooking juices with a little butter or olive oil.

8 dried morel mushrooms
1 Tbsp (15 mL) olive oil
1 Tbsp (15 mL) butter
1 leek, washed, trimmed, and thinly sliced
1 Tbsp (15 mL) finely minced garlic
¼ cup (60 mL) olives, pitted and finely diced
¼ cup (60 mL) finely diced chorizo
Salt and pepper, to taste
Vegetable stock (or dry white wine, apple cider, etc.), for cooking

Vinaigrette
1 tsp (5 mL) sweet paprika
2 Tbsp (30 mL) sherry vinegar
1 tsp (5 mL) finely minced garlic
3 Tbsp (45 mL) chopped flat-leaf parsley
2 Tbsp (30 mL) olive oil

1. Place the mushrooms in a heatproof bowl. Cover with boiling hot water and set aside. Meanwhile, warm a sauté pan over medium-high heat. Place the olive oil, butter, leek, garlic, olives, and chorizo in the pan and sauté the vegetables without browning. Remove from heat, cool slightly, and season with salt and pepper. Let cool to handling temperature.
2. Remove the mushrooms from the soaking liquid and gently squeeze dry. Place the mushrooms on a plate lined with paper towels. Using a small spoon (or clean fingers), fill each mushroom with an eighth of the chorizo mixture. Set aside.
3. In a small mixing bowl, combine the paprika, sherry vinegar, garlic, parsley, and olive oil. Whisk until smooth, then season vinaigrette with salt and pepper and set aside.
4. Place the stuffed morels in a sauté pan and add a little stock. Gently heat to warm through, about 2–3 minutes. Transfer to a serving plate and drizzle with the vinaigrette. Garnish with a few parsley sprigs and serve immediately.

JAPANESE PORK AND MUSHROOM GYOZA

MAKES 24

These addictive dumplings are easy to make in bulk and they store well in the freezer.

Gyoza

½ lb (225 g) ground pork
½ cup (125 mL) mushrooms (shiitake or button)
1 Tbsp (15 mL) minced fresh ginger
¼ cup (60 mL) finely chopped cabbage
1 tsp (5 mL) salt
1 Tbsp (15 mL) cornstarch
1 tsp (5 mL) sesame oil
1 recipe gyoza wrapper dough (see sidebar, p. 159; or pre-made wonton wrappers)
1 egg, beaten (or 2 Tbsp [30 mL] water)
1 Tbsp (15 mL) vegetable oil

Dipping sauce

¼ cup (60 mL) rice vinegar
1 Tbsp (15 mL) soy sauce
1 Tbsp (15 mL) shredded fresh ginger
1 tsp (5 mL) hot sauce

1. In a small bowl, prepare the dipping sauce by combining the vinegar, soy sauce, ginger, and hot sauce. Stir well to mix and set aside.
2. In a medium bowl, combine pork, mushrooms, ginger, cabbage, salt, cornstarch, and sesame oil. Mix until smooth and cover with plastic wrap. Chill in fridge for at least 1 hour. On a work surface, lay out 4 wrappers. Using a pastry brush, coat each round with a light covering of egg wash (or water, if using). Place 1 teaspoon (5 mL) of filling in the centre of each wrapper and fold it to form a half moon. Make sure to keep the wrapper's edges free of filling to ensure a good seal. Press edges together firmly to seal, make 3 or 4 small folds along the edge to make a pleated finish.
3. In a non-stick skillet, heat oil over medium-high, then add the gyoza and pan-fry for 1 minute. Add 1 cup (250 mL) water and cover the skillet with a lid. Cook until the moisture evaporates, about 7–8 minutes. Uncover and finish cooking dumplings until the bottoms are browned, about 2 minutes. Transfer to a plate and serve warm with the dipping sauce.

GYOZA WRAPPER DOUGH

1 cup (250 mL) unbleached flour
½ tsp (2 mL) salt
¼ cup (60 mL) boiling water

In a food processor, add the flour and salt. Turn on the processor and add the water slowly through the feed tube until the dough comes together in a ball. Remove from the processor bowl, cover in plastic wrap, and let rest for at least 1 hour and up to 3 hours. Cut the dough into 24 walnut-sized pieces, lay on a floured work surface, and roll out with a rolling pin into small rounds. Make the dough as thin as possible and about 3 inches (7.5 cm) in diameter.

SALMON AND ENOKI MUSHROOM TARTAR

SERVES 4–6

A Japanese-inspired dish that is wonderful when fresh sockeye salmon is available. Use the freshest salmon you can find. The fattiness of the fish is cut by the light mushroom flavour and the zip of the lemon and wasabi. I use a ring mould to make a nice presentation, but you can use a small can with the top and bottom lids removed for the same effect (just be careful with the sharp edges).

½ lb (225 g) sockeye salmon
3.5 oz (100 g) enoki mushrooms
1 tsp (5 mL) finely chopped capers
1 green onion, finely minced
1 tsp (5 mL) wasabi paste
1 Tbsp (15 mL) mayonnaise
Juice from half a lemon
Salt and pepper, to taste
1 Tbsp (15 mL) tobiko (flying fish roe)
Shredded nori seaweed, for garnish

1. Cut the salmon into thin slices, then cut each slice into strips. Cut the strips into a fine dice. Add to a bowl and keep chilled. Take the mushrooms and cut off the root ends, then finely dice the mushrooms, keeping the heads whole. Add to the salmon.
2. Add the capers, green onion, wasabi, mayonnaise, and lemon juice to the bowl. Stir well to mix. Taste and season with salt and pepper.
3. To serve, mound on a serving plate and top with tobiko and shredded nori. Serve with crackers or fresh baguette.

STEAMED BUNS (BAO) WITH SWEET SOY BRAISED MUSHROOMS

MAKES ABOUT 24

These buns are similar to those you find on a Chinese dim sum menu. You can add a little diced Chinese barbecue pork to the mushroom filling if you like. These buns also freeze well and can be cooked from the frozen state.

Bao dough

1½ tsp (7.5 mL) instant dry yeast
¾ cup (180 mL) lukewarm water
2 Tbsp (30 mL) canola oil
2 Tbsp (30 mL) white sugar
2 tsp (10 mL) baking powder
3 cups (750 mL) all-purpose flour

Filling

2 cups (500 mL) chopped mushrooms (shiitake, button, chanterelle, button, etc.)
1 Tbsp (15 mL) sweet soy sauce (or 1 tsp [5 mL] brown sugar plus 1 Tbsp [15 mL] soy sauce)
2 green onions, chopped
1 tsp (5 mL) hot sauce
1 Tbsp (15 mL) rice vinegar
1 garlic clove, minced

1. Place the yeast in a small bowl, then add the water and set aside for 1 minute to soften. Whisk in the oil to blend and dissolve the yeast. Set aside.
2. In a food processor, combine the sugar, baking powder, and flour and pulse to combine. With the processor running, pour the yeast mixture through the feed tube in a steady stream until the dough starts coming together into a ball, about 20 seconds. (If this doesn't happen, add more lukewarm water by the teaspoon.) Let the machine continue for 45–60 seconds to knead most of the dough into a large ball that cleans the sides of the bowl. Transfer to a floured work surface and knead lightly until smooth.
3. Lightly oil a clean bowl and add the dough. Cover with plastic wrap and place in a warm, draft-free place to rise until nearly doubled, about 30–45 minutes (timing will vary depending on the temperature of the room). You can also refrigerate the dough overnight before using.
4. In a small bowl, prepare the filling by combining the mushrooms, soy sauce, green onions, hot sauce, vinegar, and garlic. Stir well to mix. Add more salt and pepper if needed.
5. Roll the dough into a long sausage-like rope about 1½ inches thick (4 cm). Cut into 1-inch (2.5 cm) pieces. Roll each piece into a 3-inch (8 cm) round. Place 1 tablespoon (15 mL) of the filling on each round. Gather up the dough along the edges and pleat to form a top over the filling. Twist these pleats to form a spiral top to the bun, making sure the edges are firmly closed to prevent the bun from splitting. (Buns can be frozen at this stage.)
6. Cut parchment paper into 2-inch (5 cm) squares and place a bun on each piece. Add buns to the basket of a steamer tray and steam for 10 minutes. Serve warm.

WOK-FRIED CRISPY MUSHROOMS WITH GARLIC AND CHILIES

SERVES 4

A versatile technique that works with many types of mushrooms. Try it with oyster mushrooms or large slices of portobello. Feel free to add more chilies if you can handle them, or add serrano or Thai bird's eye chilies for even more heat.

2 cups (500 mL) shiitake mushroom caps (or oyster or portobello)
1 egg, whisked
3 Tbsp (45 mL) rice flour
½ cup (125 mL) oil, for frying
2 Tbsp (30 mL) chopped garlic
1 small onion, finely diced
1 jalapeno pepper, chopped
2 Tbsp (30 mL) chopped fresh cilantro
Salt and pepper, to taste

1. Place the shiitake caps in a bowl and add the whisked egg. Sprinkle the rice flour overtop and toss to coat. Place oil in a wok and heat until very hot, then add the mushrooms individually. Stir with a large spoon or spatula. Have a metal bowl containing a sieve strainer off to the side. When the mushrooms are brown, about 1 minute, remove with a slotted spoon and transfer to the strainer. Pour off all but 1 tablespoon (15 mL) of oil. Be careful, this oil will be very hot, so pour it away from your body into a wide bowl (let cool and discard).
2. Return the wok to the heat and add the garlic, onion, and jalapeno. Sauté until the onion softens and begins to brown. Add the mushrooms and cilantro and toss to coat. Season well with salt and pepper. Transfer to a plate and serve immediately.

SIDE DISHES

MUSHROOM BREAD PUDDING FROM RECIPE ON PAGE 170

TRUFFLED POTATO GRATIN

MAKES 12 PORTIONS

Truffles work their magic when paired with background flavours like potatoes and cream. This dish combines both to create a classic and tasty side dish, particularly with beef or lamb. The dish is also excellent with dried porcini or morel mushrooms.

2 cups (500 mL) milk (or half-and-half)
1 Tbsp (15 mL) minced garlic
1 Tbsp (15 mL) minced fresh sage
1 Tbsp (15 mL) minced fresh rosemary
1 tsp (5 mL) truffle paste (or truffle oil)
Salt and pepper, to taste
2 lb (1 kg) potatoes
1 cup (250 mL) grated cheese (cheddar, Swiss, etc.)

1. Preheat the oven to 350°F (180°C).
2. In a saucepan, combine the milk, garlic, sage, rosemary, truffle paste, salt, and pepper. Bring to a boil, then reduce heat and let infuse for 15 minutes.
3. Peel the potatoes, then wash them and cut very thinly with a mandoline. Place a sieve over a small casserole dish and strain a ladleful (1 cup [125 mL]) of the infused milk into it. Add a layer of potato slices to the dish and keep adding layers along with a little milk between them until the potato is used up. Top with cheese and place in the oven. Bake for 45 minutes, or until the potato is soft and the cheese is golden brown. Let cool to room temperature. For best results, refrigerate for at least 2 hours, then cut into wedges and reheat in a hot oven for 10 minutes.

PORCINI MACARONI AND CHEESE

SERVES 6

A luxurious version of a classic comfort food. It is excellent with button mushrooms heightened with the essence of porcini powder. If you use fresh porcini or chanterelles, don't place them in the pasta water. Instead, sauté the mushrooms in a little butter and add to the béchamel sauce. This dish is also great with a spoonful of truffle paste added at the end.

1 recipe porcini béchamel sauce (p. 224)
1 cup (250 mL) grated mozzarella cheese
¼ cup (60 mL) grated Parmesan cheese
2 cups (500 mL) uncooked macaroni
2 cups (500 mL) trimmed broccoli florets
2 cups (500 mL) diced button mushrooms (or porcini, chanterelle, etc.)
1 cup (250 mL) cubed ham (optional)
1 cup (250 mL) grated Gruyère cheese (or Swiss cheese)

1. Preheat the oven to 350°F (180°C).
2. Prepare the béchamel according to the directions. Add the mozzarella and Parmesan cheeses and stir until smooth. Keep warm until needed.
3. Heat a large pot of salted water. When it starts boiling, add the pasta and stir to keep the pasta from sticking to the bottom. The pot will foam. Turn down the heat to obtain a rolling simmer. Add a little oil if the pot continues to foam excessively. Cook the pasta for 5 minutes and then add the broccoli and mushrooms to the pasta. Cook for a further 3 minutes or until the pasta is al dente, cooked through but with a little bite.
4. Strain pasta and vegetables. Transfer to a casserole dish. Add the béchamel and ham (if using), stirring well to coat. Top with the Gruyère and bake in the oven for 20 minutes, or until the cheese is golden brown on top and bubbling. Remove from the oven and serve warm.

WARM BACON, CHANTERELLE, AND POTATO SALAD

SERVES 6–8

A variation on a classic German potato salad made with chanterelles. It is best to add the dressing to warm potatoes so they soak up all the dressing. Serve at room temperature.

2 lb (1 kg) potatoes, peeled
¼ lb (115 g) thick-cut bacon, cut in thin strips
1 lb (450 g) chanterelles, cleaned and sliced
Salt and pepper, to taste
2 Tbsp (30 mL) apple cider vinegar
2 Tbsp (30 mL) olive oil
2 Tbsp (30 mL) grainy mustard
1 tsp (5 mL) chopped capers
3 Tbsp (45 mL) chopped sweet onion (or green onion)
Fresh chives or green onions, minced, for garnish

1. Add potatoes to a large pot of salted cold water. Bring to a boil and cook until tender.
2. Meanwhile, warm a skillet over medium-high heat, add the bacon, and heat until the bacon is browned and has rendered its fat. Add the chanterelles and sauté until the mushrooms give off moisture and it has completely evaporated. Season with salt and pepper. When the mushrooms just begin to brown on the edges, remove from heat and set aside.
3. In a large mixing bowl, combine vinegar, oil, mustard, capers, and onion. Stir until mixed. Drain potatoes and add while still warm to the dressing. Add the bacon and toss to coat. Serve warm, garnished with fresh chives or green onions.

MUSHROOM BREAD PUDDING

MAKES 8 PORTIONS

Savoury bread pudding is great on its own with a side salad for lunch or dinner. It also makes a great base for meat or poultry dishes, particularly those that have a braised sauce. You can use almost any mushroom or combination of mushrooms for this dish. It is a good choice for softer mushrooms like morels, winter chanterelles, and fairy ring mushrooms.

1 cup (250 mL) diced bacon
2 leeks, trimmed, washed, and sliced
2 cups (500 mL) chopped mushrooms (porcini, morel, button, etc.)
2 Tbsp (30 mL) minced mixed fresh herbs (rosemary, sage, thyme)
1 Tbsp (15 mL) minced garlic
Salt and pepper, to taste
6 large eggs
4 cups (1 L) milk (or half-and-half or whipping cream)
6 cups (1.5 L) thinly sliced French bread or baguette
1 cup (250 mL) grated sharp cheese (Gruyère, white cheddar, Gouda, etc.)

1. Preheat the oven to 325°F (160°C).
2. In a sauté pan, add the bacon and sauté to reduce the fat, pouring off some of the fat if a large quantity is rendered. Add the leeks and mushrooms and sauté until soft. Add the herbs and garlic, seasoning well with salt and pepper. Sauté until fragrant, remove from heat, and set aside.
3. In a mixing bowl, add the eggs and whisk to mix. Add the milk and whisk well to blend. Season well with salt and pepper.
4. Place a layer of bread in a large, buttered casserole dish. Sprinkle a little of the bacon and leek mixture overtop, then repeat with the remaining bread and seasoning. Pour the egg mixture over the bread, pushing down with a spoon to ensure all the slices are soaked with the mixture. Scatter the cheese overtop and place in the oven for 45 minutes, or until set and slightly browned on top. Remove from the oven and let stand for at least 10 minutes. Cut into squares (or scoop with a large spoon) and serve warm.

SOFT MUSHROOM POLENTA

MAKES 6–8

I prefer my polenta soft and rich. This version delivers with a soft kiss of butter and cream. It's a dish that you can use just about any mushroom with. Morels, porcini, pine mushrooms, and cauliflower fungi would be my top choices, but any cultivated mushroom would also work well. To throw it over the top, you can add some truffle paste to the final mix.

1 Tbsp (15 mL) olive oil
¼ cup (60 mL) minced shallots
2 cups (500 mL) diced assorted mushrooms
4 cups (1 L) chicken stock
1¼ cups (310 mL) polenta
Sea salt and pepper, to taste
¼ cup (60 mL) salted butter
½ cup (125 mL) grated Parmesan cheese
¼ cup (60 mL) whipping cream
1 tsp (5 mL) truffle paste (optional)

1. Heat a heavy saucepan over medium. Add the olive oil, shallots, and mushrooms. Heat until the shallots and mushrooms soften. Add the stock and bring to a boil. Add the polenta while whisking to blend. Reduce heat to a low simmer. Stir polenta occasionally with a wooden spoon for about 20–30 minutes. Stir in salt, pepper, butter, Parmesan, and whipping cream. Keep warm and let stand for at least 10 minutes. Before serving, add truffle paste and thin to a soft texture with a little stock or cream. Check seasoning and serve warm.

RICE, GRAINS, AND BEANS

RICE CONGEE FROM RECIPE ON PAGE 180

SHIITAKE SUSHI RICE

SERVES 4–6

One of the best kitchen investments I ever made was my rice cooker. It is a small, Japanese countertop model and it makes perfect rice every time. It is highly recommended for cooking rice, barley, and other grains. This recipe is for stovetop rice, but will give great results with a rice cooker. Make sure to keep the temperature low, barely a simmer, and let stand with the lid on tightly for at least 15 minutes.

1 cup (250 mL) sushi rice
2 cups (500 mL) water
4 dried shiitake mushrooms
2 Tbsp (30 mL) rice vinegar
1 tsp (5 mL) white sugar
1 tsp (5 mL) salt

1. Using a medium pot with a tight-fitting lid, add the rice and rinse under cold running water, rubbing to release the starch. Rinse until the water becomes relatively clear. Drain, and add the measured water and shiitake mushrooms. Bring to a boil over high heat. Reduce the heat to low, cover, and cook for 20 minutes. Remove the pot from the heat and let stand for 15 minutes.
2. Place the vinegar, sugar, and salt in a small bowl. Stir well to mix. Turn the rice out into a large baking sheet (or bowl). Retrieve the shiitakes, cutting off their stems and mincing the caps finely (discard the stems). Sprinkle the mushrooms over the rice and add the vinegar mixture. With a wooden utensil, stir the rice until it is well mixed and beginning to cool. Cover with a clean towel and keep at room temperature until needed.

CASSOULET WITH MUSHROOMS, BACON CUBES, AND SAUSAGE

SERVES 6–8

A country-style, rib-sticking dish from the south of France. You will be rewarded by seeking out good local artisan-made bacon and sausages. Traditionally you can put a chunk of duck or goose confit in the casserole, which will add even more richness to the party.

- 2 cups (500 mL) dried small white (navy) beans
- 6 cups (1.5 L) duck, chicken, or mushroom stock
- 2 carrots, peeled and chopped
- 1 onion, chopped
- 2 celery stalks, trimmed and chopped
- 1 Tbsp (15 mL) minced garlic
- 1 Tbsp (15 mL) minced fresh rosemary
- 1 Tbsp (15 mL) minced fresh sage
- 2 dried bay leaves
- 2 cups (500 mL) smoked sausage, cut into chunks
- 1 lb (450 g) slab bacon, cut into large cubes
- 1 Tbsp (15 mL) olive oil
- 2 cups (500 mL) sliced fresh mushrooms (chanterelle, porcini, button, etc.)
- Salt and pepper, to taste
- 1 cup (250 mL) dried breadcrumbs
- 1 Tbsp (15 mL) minced garlic
- 1 Tbsp (15 mL) chopped fresh parsley
- Olive oil, for drizzling

1. Place dried beans in a large container. Cover with water and refrigerate overnight. The next day, drain and rinse the beans. (Doing so helps to soften the beans and remove indigestible enzymes.)
2. Add the drained beans to a large pot and cover with water. Cook for 1 hour, or until the beans begin to soften and become tender. (The exact time will depend on the freshness of the beans.) Drain the beans and return to the pot. Add the stock, carrots, onion, celery, garlic, rosemary, sage, and bay leaves. Bring to a simmer and add the sausage and bacon. Simmer for 1 hour or until the beans are very tender and the bacon is soft. Transfer the beans and meat to a large roasting tray. Set aside to cool. Preheat the oven to 350°F (180°C).
3. In a sauté pan over medium-high heat, add the olive oil and sauté the mushrooms until lightly browned. Add to the bean mixture and stir. Taste the beans and adjust seasoning with salt and pepper, adding a little more stock or water if the beans appear too dry. In a bowl, combine the breadcrumbs, garlic, and parsley. Drizzle with olive oil until the mixture comes together in a clump. Sprinkle the seasoned breadcrumbs overtop of the beans and place in the oven. Bake for 40 minutes, or until the topping is browned. Serve with good crusty bread.

MUSHROOM-CRUSTED ALBACORE TUNA WITH SHIITAKE SUSHI SALAD

SERVES 4

Tuna is fantastic with mushrooms, particularly if you leave the tuna very rare in the middle. The outside will char and be crusted with the shiitake mushroom powder. Albacore tuna is the most sustainable type in the marketplace. This technique for searing the tuna is called *tataki* in Japan, named after the pounded ginger paste the dish is traditionally served with.

½ lb (225 g) albacore tuna loin
1 Tbsp (15 mL) shiitake powder (p. 73)
1 Tbsp (15 mL) light soy sauce
1 tsp (5 mL) honey
1 tsp (5 mL) sesame oil
1 Tbsp (15 mL) grapeseed oil
1 tsp (5 mL) wasabi paste
Zest and juice of 1 lime
1 tsp (5 mL) honey
2 Tbsp (30 mL) minced pickled ginger
3 Tbsp (45 mL) mayonnaise
1 recipe shiitake sushi rice (p. 174)
1 cup (250 mL) seeded and julienned cucumber
3.5 oz (100 g) enoki mushrooms, for garnish
Toasted sesame seeds, for garnish

1. In a glass container, place the tuna loin and sprinkle with the shiitake powder, soy sauce, honey, and sesame oil. Roll the loin to completely cover in seasoning. Let stand for 10 minutes to allow the flavours to penetrate. Heat a skillet over medium-high. When very hot, add the grapeseed oil and tuna and sear until the outside starts to char. Rotate tuna so each side gets a little char but the centre is still raw. Transfer to a plate and set aside to rest.
2. In a mixing bowl, combine the wasabi, lime zest and juice, honey, pickled ginger, and mayonnaise. Whisk to combine, taste and adjust seasoning with more wasabi, if desired. (This sauce can also be made in a blender to create a smooth purée.)
3. On a serving platter, mound the shiitake sushi rice. Scatter the cucumber on top of the rice. Cut the tuna into rounds and place on top of the cucumber and rice. Drizzle the dressing over the rice and tuna. Garnish with enoki mushrooms and a sprinkling of sesame seeds.

MUSHROOM, PROSCIUTTO, AND BARLEY PILAF

SERVES 4

Barley is a nutritious grain that is often underutilized. It will take about 40 minutes to cook. Grains dehydrate over time so old grains may need a little more time to absorb the cooking liquid and soften. Buy grains from a bulk-food store with good turnover to ensure a fresh product. Beef or chicken stock makes a richly flavoured dish. However, vegetable or mushroom stock will also produce excellent results.

1½ cups (375 mL) pearl barley
1 Tbsp (15 mL) olive oil
1 Tbsp (15 mL) minced garlic
½ cup (125 mL) peeled and sliced shallots
2 cups (500 mL) cubed mushrooms (chanterelle, morel, porcini, oyster, pine mushroom, etc.)
Salt and pepper, to taste
4 cups (1 L) beef or chicken stock (or boiling water)
4 slices prosciutto ham, thinly sliced and minced
2 Tbsp (30 mL) fresh Italian parsley (or basil)
2 Tbsp (30 mL) grated Parmesan cheese

1. In a sieve, rinse the barley under cold running water. Place the strainer in a pot of cold water and let stand for 5 minutes.
2. In a heavy-bottomed saucepan with a tight-fitting lid, heat olive oil over high for 45 seconds. Add the garlic, shallots, and mushrooms and season well with salt and pepper. Add the barley and stock. Bring to a boil, cover, and reduce heat to low. Cook for 30 minutes, stirring occasionally. The barley should be tender but still a little firm.
3. Remove from the heat and let stand, covered, for an additional 10 minutes. Add the prosciutto, parsley, and cheese. Stir to mix and serve warm.

PINE MUSHROOM RISOTTO WITH SEAWEED, SOYBEANS, AND PINE NUTS

SERVES 4

This recipe is amazing with BC pine mushrooms. If they are not in season, try a mixture of button, cremini, oyster, and shiitake mushrooms. Many types of dried seaweed will work in the dish. Soak the seaweed in water for 20 minutes, then chop finely with a sharp knife. Both seaweed and mushrooms are rich in umami and antioxidants.

4 cups (1 L) chicken or mushroom stock
¼ cup (60 mL) finely chopped dried seaweed (bull kelp, dulse, nori, etc.)
2 Tbsp (30 mL) grapeseed oil
1½ cups (375 mL) arborio rice
1 cup (250 mL) dry white wine
1 Tbsp (15 mL) minced garlic
1 cup (250 mL) cleaned and diced pine mushrooms
1 Tbsp (15 mL) Japanese soy sauce (with added seaweed and dashi, if possible)
1 cup (250 mL) shelled fresh soybeans (edamame)
2 Tbsp (30 mL) butter (optional; or 1 tsp [5 mL] sesame oil)
Salt and pepper, to taste
¼ cup (60 mL) toasted pine nuts
1 green onion, finely minced

1. In a saucepan, combine the stock and chopped seaweed. Bring to a boil, then reduce the heat and keep warm.
2. Warm a heavy-bottomed saucepan over medium-high heat, add the oil and rice. Stir until the rice turns translucent and begins to stick to the bottom. Add the wine, garlic, and mushrooms and stir until the wine is almost evaporated. Add the stock 1 cup (250 mL) at a time, stirring frequently until the liquid you have added is absorbed. Reduce heat if it cooks too quickly.
3. Continue adding stock until the rice is tender with a bit of bite left in the centre. Add the soy sauce, soybeans, and butter. Stir to mix and season well with salt and pepper. Transfer to serving bowls and garnish with the pine nuts and green onion.

RICE CONGEE WITH PINE MUSHROOMS, BRAISED GREENS, AND SPICED PORK

SERVES 4–6

This dish is delicious with pine mushrooms but is also great with shiitakes, button mushrooms, shimeji, and enoki mushrooms. When you sauté the meat and greens you can reserve a little to spoon on top of the rice as a garnish. You can also use brown rice or barley, just purée with a hand blender before adding the meat to get the right (thicker) texture.

1 lb (450 g) ground pork (or chicken or turkey)
2 Tbsp (30 mL) rice flour
1 tsp (5 mL) grated fresh ginger
1 tsp (5 mL) five-spice powder
1 tsp (5 mL) salt
6 cups (1.5 L) chicken or mushroom stock
2 cups (500 mL) short-grained rice
1 Tbsp (15 mL) grapeseed oil
1 cup (250 mL) sliced pine mushrooms (or any mushroom)
1 Tbsp (15 mL) chopped garlic
1 Tbsp (15 mL) hoisin sauce
1 tsp (5 mL) sesame oil
4 cups (1 L) chopped fresh greens (kale, spinach, sui choy, bok choy, etc.)
Salt and pepper, to taste
Fresh cilantro leaves, for garnish

1. In a bowl, combine the ground pork, rice flour, ginger, five-spice powder, and salt. Mix with your hands until a smooth paste is formed. Set aside until needed.
2. In a stockpot, bring the stock to a boil. Add the rice, reduce the heat to a simmer, and cook for at least 40 minutes, or until the rice is very soft and the congee has thickened considerably.
3. Warm a sauté pan over medium-high heat. Add the oil and heat until almost smoking. Add the marinated pork and sauté it, breaking up the chunks of meat. Let brown on one side before tossing to again to break up the meat into small grains. Add the pine mushrooms, garlic, hoisin sauce, sesame oil, and greens. Sauté until the greens wilt. Pour the mixture into the rice congee. Taste and correct seasoning with salt and pepper.
4. Transfer to serving bowls and garnish with fresh cilantro leaves.

CHANTERELLE BAKED BEANS

MAKES 6–8 PORTIONS

An excellent side dish for the barbecue or to warm the cool nights of fall. The chanterelles add a great texture to the beans. Works great with cultivated mushrooms as well, particularly shiitakes and shimeji mushrooms.

1 lb (450 g) dried small white (navy) beans
½ tsp (2 mL) ground cloves
1 medium onion, peeled and diced
1 celery stalk, diced
2 garlic cloves, minced
1 bay leaf
6 slices thick-cut bacon, chopped
2 cups (500 mL) chopped chanterelle mushrooms
1 tsp (5 mL) salt
¼ cup (60 mL) ketchup
¼ cup (60 mL) molasses
3 Tbsp (45 mL) apple cider vinegar
2 tsp (10 mL) dry mustard powder
1 tsp (5 mL) hot sauce

1. Place dried beans in a large container. Cover with water and refrigerate overnight. The next day, drain and rinse the beans. Add them to a large pot and cover with water. Add the cloves, onion, celery, garlic, and bay leaf. Bring to a boil. Reduce the heat and simmer for 1–2 hours, or until the beans are just tender. (Older beans will take longer to cook.) Add more water to the beans if the water level drops below the top of the beans. Preheat oven to 350°F (180°C).
2. Warm a large skillet over medium heat. Add the bacon and cook until it browns and renders some of the fat. Add the chanterelles and sauté until the mushrooms loose their moisture. Scrape the mixture into a large casserole dish, then add the bean mixture and stir to mix. Add the salt, ketchup, molasses, cider vinegar, dry mustard, and hot sauce. Stir and place in the oven for 1 hour. Serve warm, even better the next day when reheated.

SOUPS AND CHOWDERS

MOREL AND STINGING NETTLE SOUP FROM RECIPE ON PAGE 188

MISO SOUP WITH MUSHROOMS AND SEAWEED

SERVES 4

This soup is packed with umami from the mushrooms and the seaweed. It is very easy to make and perfect for a quick meal and for impressing guests at a dinner party. Many of the Asian cultivated mushrooms like shiitake, maitake, shimeji, enoki, and pom pom are excellent in this soup and add a great boost to your immune system.

4 cups (1 L) dashi stock (see sidebar)
2 Tbsp (30 mL) shiro (light) miso paste
10 oz (300 g) package soft tofu, diced
2 cups (500 mL) sliced mushrooms
2 Tbsp (30 mL) shredded seaweed, soaked in cold water
1 green onion, thinly sliced

1. In a medium stockpot over high heat, combine the stock and miso. Bring to a boil, then reduce to a simmer. Add the tofu, mushrooms, and seaweed. Simmer for 5 minutes. To serve, divide the soup among 4 bowls and sprinkle the onion overtop.

Dashi Stock

Made from bonito flakes and seaweed, this stock is a staple of Japanese cuisine. Bonito flakes and kombu are found in most Japanese stores. You can also find instant dashi stock in many grocery stores.

4 cups (1 L) water
1 oz (28 g) kombu (bull kelp) seaweed
¼ cup (60 mL) dried bonito flakes

Place water and seaweed in a stockpot. Bring to a boil and then remove from heat. Reserve the kombu for another use (such as including in soup—just cut into thin strips). Add the bonito flakes to the seaweed broth and let steep for about 5 minutes. Strain the stock and use the same day, discarding the used bonito flakes.

HEIRLOOM TOMATO AND PINE MUSHROOM SOUP

SERVES 6

The richness of tomato soup is a perfect vehicle for showcasing the charms of pine mushrooms. If you don't have access to pine mushrooms, you can also use button or cauliflower mushrooms.

2 lb (1 kg) ripe heirloom tomatoes
4 cups (1 L) chicken or mushroom stock
1 cup (250 mL) peeled and diced onions
1 cup (250 mL) diced celery
1 cup (250 mL) sliced pine mushrooms (or button mushrooms)
2 Tbsp (30 mL) minced fresh sage
2 Tbsp (30 mL) cornstarch (or tapioca starch)
Salt and pepper, to taste
¼ cup (60 mL) sour cream
1 Tbsp (15 mL) good balsamic vinegar

1. Bring a large pot of water to a boil. Core the tomatoes and cut an X in the bottom of each one. Add them to the boiling water and poach until their skins begin to curl off at the cuts, about 1–2 minutes. Transfer to a bowl of cold water. Peel off the skins completely and set tomatoes aside.
2. In a stockpot, add the stock, peeled tomatoes, onions, and celery. Bring to a boil, then simmer for 20 minutes, or until the vegetables are tender. Purée the soup with a hand blender (or use a blender or food processor) until smooth. Bring back to a boil and add the pine mushrooms and sage. Mix the starch with an equal amount of water. Pour into the boiling soup, whisking until it thickens. Season well with salt and pepper.
3. In a small bowl, mix the sour cream and balsamic vinegar. Whisk until the mixture is smooth—it can be thinned with a little water if it appears too thick. To serve, transfer hot soup to a bowl and drizzle with the cream mixture.

SWEET CORN CHOWDER WITH PORCINI MUSHROOMS

SERVES 4–6

A great dish for late summer when the corn and porcini seasons overlap. You can add the corncobs to the stock, bring to a boil, and simmer to extract a fuller corn flavour. Remove the cobs before proceeding with the recipe. This recipe also works well with dried porcini (2 ounces [60 g]) that have been presoaked in water.

1 Tbsp (15 mL) olive oil
1 Tbsp (15 mL) butter
1 onion, peeled and diced
2 cups (500 mL) fresh porcini mushrooms (or chanterelle or button mushrooms)
1 Tbsp (15 mL) minced garlic
4 cups (1 L) chicken stock
4 fresh corn ears
1 large potato, peeled and diced
1 large carrot, peeled and diced
1 cup (250 mL) whipping cream
Salt and pepper, to taste

1. In a large pot, add the olive oil and butter and heat over medium-high. Add the onion and sauté for 1–2 minutes. Add the mushrooms and garlic and cook until the mixture softens but does not brown, reducing the heat down if it begins to brown too quickly. Add the chicken stock and bring to a simmer.
2. Cut the kernels off the corn ears and add to the pot. Bring to a boil, then reduce the heat and simmer for 20 minutes. With an immersion blender (or countertop blender) purée the soup until a smooth consistency is reached. Add the potato and carrot and cook for 7–8 minutes, or until just tender. Before serving, add the whipping cream and season well with salt and pepper.

MOREL AND STINGING NETTLE SOUP

SERVES 4

Stinging nettles are a symbol of spring harvests in many parts of the world. The plant is used as a medicinal tonic and is reputed to boost the immune system and purge the body of toxins accumulated over a long winter of relative inactivity. This soup is perfect with morels but any cultivated mushroom will work nicely.

2 oz (60 g) dried morels
4 cups (1 L) fresh stinging nettle tips
4 cups (1 L) chicken or vegetable stock
½ cup (125 mL) whipping cream
Sea salt and pepper, to taste
1 cup (250 mL) sour cream (or yogurt)
2 Tbsp (30 mL) lemon juice
1 Tbsp (15 mL) butter
2 Tbsp (30 mL) chopped garlic
1 Tbsp (15 mL) chopped fresh chives

1. Soak the morels in warm water for 1 hour. Remove morels, squeeze out the moisture, and slice into rounds.
2. Bring a pot of water to a boil and add the nettles. Cook for 5 minutes and then strain. Let cool and squeeze out all the moisture. Chop coarsely.
3. In a small stockpot over medium-high heat, bring the stock to a boil. Add the nettles and bring back to a boil. Using an immersion blender, purée the nettles until smooth. Alternatively, process in batches in a blender or food processor until the fine purée is obtained. Add the whipping cream and stir to mix. Season with salt and pepper.
4. In a small bowl, mix together the sour cream and lemon juice. Mix and chill until needed.
5. In a sauté pan over medium-high heat, add the butter and heat until sizzling. Add the morels and garlic. Sauté for 2–3 minutes, or until the morels begin to brown. To serve, bring nettle soup back to a boil, then transfer to serving bowls and top with a spoonful of sour cream and a spoonful of morels. Garnish with chives and serve hot.

LEEK AND POTATO SOUP WITH MORELS AND HAM

SERVES 4–6

A springtime soup that can be made with fresh or dried morels. Russet potatoes are best for this soup as they make a light purée. The ham should be a quality country-style ham with a good smoke level. Mince the ham finely to distribute it throughout the soup.

4 large russet potatoes, peeled, cleaned, and cubed
2 leeks, washed and sliced
8 cups (2 L) chicken or vegetable stock
2 Tbsp (30 mL) chopped fresh thyme
1 medium onion, peeled and chopped
1 stalk celery, chopped
1 Tbsp (15 mL) minced garlic
¼ cup (60 mL) cream (optional)
Salt and pepper, to taste
½ cup (125 mL) minced ham
1 cup (250 mL) sliced morel mushrooms
Sour cream, for garnish
Fresh chives or parsley, chopped, for garnish

1. Place potatoes and leeks in a stockpot and add the stock, thyme, onion, celery, and garlic. Bring to a boil, then reduce to a simmer and cook for 30 minutes. Purée the soup with a hand blender (or purée in batches with a blender or food processor). Add cream (if using), then check the seasoning and adjust with salt and pepper.
2. Add the ham and sliced morels and simmer for 10 minutes more. To serve, ladle soup into bowls and drizzle with sour cream. Garnish with fresh chives or parsley.

WINTER SQUASH SOUP WITH CAULIFLOWER MUSHROOMS

SERVES 4–6

I love to make this soup with Japanese kabocha squash. The flesh is sweet and deep orange. If you can't find this variety, try to get a buttercup squash. The cauliflower mushroom is amazing in this soup, but pine mushrooms and oyster mushrooms also work well.

1 large winter squash, peeled, cleaned, and cubed
1 Tbsp (15 mL) olive oil
Salt and pepper, to taste
8 cups (2 L) chicken stock, water, or apple juice
2 Tbsp (30 mL) chopped fresh sage
1 cup (250 mL) peeled and chopped onions
1 stalk celery, chopped
1 Tbsp (15 mL) minced garlic
1 tsp (5 mL) ground allspice
1 cup (250 mL) cream or sour cream (optional)
1 Tbsp (15 mL) salted butter or olive oil
2 cups (500 mL) chopped cauliflower mushrooms
Fresh chives or sage, chopped, for ganish

1. Preheat the oven to 350°F (180°C).
2. Place the squash on a baking tray and drizzle with olive oil and salt and pepper. Place in the oven for 30 minutes, or until soft and just starting to brown.
3. Transfer the squash to a soup pot and cover with stock, water, or juice. Add the sage, onions, celery, garlic, and allspice. Bring to a boil, then reduce to a simmer and cook for 30 minutes. Purée the soup with a hand blender (or purée in batches with a blender or food processor). Add the cream (if using), then check the seasoning and adjust with salt and pepper.
4. In a sauté pan, over medium-high heat, add the butter or oil and sauté the mushrooms until they release their juices and begin to brown. Season with salt and pepper. To serve, ladle soup into bowls and top with a spoonful or two of the sautéed mushrooms. For a nice effect, drizzle a little cream or sour cream on top of the soup and garnish with fresh chives or chopped sage.

CURRIED MUSHROOM AND COCONUT BISQUE

SERVES 6–8

Chanterelles are excellent in this soup, but a wide variety of wild and cultivated mushrooms will also work. Oyster and shimeji mushrooms are particularly delicious. This dish can be kept as a vegetarian soup, or you can add chopped cooked chicken or turkey.

1 Tbsp (15 mL) grapeseed (or vegetable) oil
2 large carrots, peeled and diced
1 stalk celery, diced
1 large onion, peeled and diced
4 cups (1 L) diced assorted mushrooms
Salt and pepper, to taste
1 Tbsp (15 mL) curry paste (or powder)
8 cups (2 L) vegetable or chicken stock
4 slices fresh ginger, minced
2 Tbsp (30 mL) chopped garlic
1 stalk lemon grass, trimmed and split
1 bunch fresh cilantro, chopped
Zest and juice of 1 lime
13 oz (385 mL) coconut milk
3 Tbsp (45 mL) cornstarch
Fresh basil leaves (Italian or Thai), chopped
Fresh bean sprouts, for garnish
Lime wedges, for garnish

1. In a stockpot, add the oil and then the carrots, celery, onion, and mushrooms. Sauté until they begin to brown, then season with salt and pepper and add the curry paste. Stir to mix. Add the stock, ginger, garlic, lemon grass, cilantro stems (reserve the leaves), lime zest and juice, and coconut milk. Bring to a boil, then reduce to a simmer and cook for 10 minutes.
2. Mix the cornstarch with 3 tablespoons (45 mL) cold water and slowly whisk into the hot soup. The mixture will thicken as it heats. Add more starch if you like a thicker soup. Serve hot, garnished with basil, reserved cilantro leaves, and bean sprouts. Squeeze the lime wedge overtop just before eating.

LAMB AND BROWN RICE SOUP WITH CHOPPED GREENS

SERVES 6–8

A great soup to follow up a leg of lamb dinner. The rice adds a heartiness that is tailor-made for the cool days of fall and winter. I really like the combination of button mushrooms and dried porcini, but many mushrooms will work in this soup.

8 cups (2 L) lamb stock
1 Tbsp (15 mL) minced garlic
2 cups (500 mL) diced button mushrooms
2 Tbsp (30 mL) rehydrated and chopped dried porcini mushrooms
1 cup (250 mL) diced onions
1 cup (250 mL) diced celery
1 cup (250 mL) peeled and diced carrots
1 cup (250 mL) brown rice, rinsed
1 cup (250 mL) finely chopped cooked lamb meat (or ground lamb meat or sausage)
Salt and pepper, to taste
4 cups (1 L) chopped greens (kale, mustard greens, arugula, etc.)
1 Tbsp (15 mL) finely chopped fresh parsley, for garnish

1. In a small stockpot, add the lamb stock, garlic, button mushrooms, dried porcini, onions, celery, carrots, and rice. Bring to a boil, then reduce the heat and cook for 30 minutes, or until the vegetables are tender.
2. Remove as much fat as possible from the cooked lamb. Add to the soup and bring the broth back to a simmer, then season well with salt and pepper. Add the greens and stir to wilt, about 3–4 minutes. Ladle the hot soup into bowls, garnish with parsley, and serve immediately.

POLISH MUSHROOM CHOWDER

SERVES 6–8

This chowder works well with many types of wild mushrooms. Choose mushrooms that have a dense texture and won't break down too much when cooked. The soup freezes well and can be portioned into meal-sized containers for future use. Potato starch is available in health food stores and is sometimes labelled potato flour.

2 Tbsp (30 mL) olive oil (or butter)
1 onion, diced
1 cup (250 mL) diced polish sausage (optional)
4 cups (1 L) diced mushrooms (chanterelle, porcini, button, hedgehog, pine mushroom, etc.)
2 Tbsp (30 mL) minced garlic
1 cup (250 mL) peeled and diced potatoes
1 celery stalk, diced
2 carrots, peeled and diced
3 Tbsp (45 mL) potato starch (or cornstarch or rice flour)
2 cups (500 mL) mushroom or vegetable stock
2 cups (500 mL) milk
1 Tbsp (15 mL) chopped fresh rosemary
1 Tbsp (15 mL) chopped fresh sage
Salt and pepper, to taste
Fresh parsley, chopped, for garnish

1. In a stockpot, heat oil over high heat for 30 seconds. Add the onion and sausage, then sauté for 3–4 minutes. Add the mushrooms and garlic, sautéing until mushrooms are soft and appear dry. Reduce heat to medium and toss in the potatoes, celery, and carrots. Continue to cook for 5–6 minutes.
2. Sprinkle the starch overtop of the vegetables and stir well to mix. Cook for 2–3 minutes and then add stock, milk, rosemary, and sage. Stir well to dissolve the flour. Bring the mixture to a boil. Reduce the heat to a simmer and cook for 10 minutes, or until the vegetables are tender. Season well with salt and pepper. Ladle the soup into soup bowls, garnish with parsley, and serve immediately.

SALADS

WILD MUSHROOM SALAD FROM RECIPE ON PAGE 198

MIXED GREENS WITH ENOKI MUSHROOMS, AVOCADO, AND CUCUMBER

SERVES 4

Buy fresh, local salad greens if possible. Wash the greens and dry with a salad spinner, or roll up in a clean tea towel. This salad is excellent with Asian greens like mizuna, mitsuba, and tatsoi. You can also use spinach with good results. Assemble this salad just before serving.

1 tsp (5 mL) sesame oil
1 tsp (5 mL) yellow mustard
1 tsp (5 mL) wasabi paste
1 Tbsp (15 mL) light soy sauce
1 Tbsp (15 mL) grapeseed oil
1 cup (250 mL) cubed seedless cucumber (English or Persian)
1 ripe avocado, peeled, cored, and diced
½ lb (225 g) mixed salad greens, washed and dried
3.5 oz (100 g) enoki mushrooms
2 Tbsp (30 mL) sesame seeds

1. In a mixing bowl, combine the sesame oil, mustard, wasabi, soy sauce, and grapeseed oil. Whisk to mix and set dressing aside.
2. Add the cucumber and avocado to the dressing. Top with the salad greens and enoki mushrooms. Just before serving, toss the salad and sprinkle the sesame seeds overtop. Serve immediately.

ROASTED PORTOBELLO WITH BACON AND FRISÉE SALAD AND PARMESAN CROUTONS

SERVES 4

Frisée (chicory) is a bitter endive that has been blanched (whitened) in the core. The outer leaves are tied up to keep sunlight off the interior. Matching this green with bacon is a classic combination that works to brighten the mushroom below. This also works well with a fresh parasol (*Lepiota*) mushroom that has opened up.

4 large portobello mushrooms
2 Tbsp (30 mL) olive oil
2 Tbsp (30 mL) minced garlic
Salt and pepper, to taste
4 slices thick-cut bacon, cut into strips
2 slices crusty bread, cut in small cubes
2 green onions, minced
2 cups (500 mL) frisée lettuce (or baby mixed greens)
1 tsp (5 mL) dry white wine vinegar
1 tsp (5 mL) olive oil
2 Tbsp (30 mL) freshly grated Parmesan cheese

1. Preheat the oven to 350°F (180°C).
2. Remove the stems from the mushrooms and scoop out the gills. Place on a baking tray and drizzle with olive oil and garlic. Season well with salt and pepper and then place in the oven. Roast for 10 minutes or until the mushrooms are browned and beginning to soften. Remove from the oven, transfer to a plate, and allow to cool slightly.
3. Meanwhile, warm a skillet over medium-high heat and add the bacon. Sauté until the bacon is crispy and has rendered fat. Add the bread cubes and sauté until the bread crisps and absorbs the bacon fat. Add the green onions and toss to coat. Transfer to a plate lined with paper towels to absorb excess fat.
4. In a bowl, add the frisée lettuce and drizzle with vinegar and olive oil. Season with salt and pepper. To serve, place the mushrooms on a plate and mound the salad on top. Sprinkle with the bacon and crouton mixture and a grating of fresh Parmesan cheese. Serve immediately.

WILD MUSHROOM SALAD WITH CAULIFLOWER, DILL, AND ROSEHIP VINAIGRETTE

SERVES 4

Rosehip butter is packed full of nutrients and vitamin C. You may have to search a little to find it in health food stores or in specialty food shops catering to Germanic and Nordic clients. Alternately, you can find rosehip syrup in some stores and it makes an acceptable substitute for the butter. You can also use apple butter or even orange marmalade as a nice substitute. We make our own rosehip butter on Deerholme Farm every late fall, just after the frost has touched the rosehips.

1 cauliflower head, cut into chunks
3 Tbsp (45 mL) apple cider vinegar, divided
1 Tbsp (15 mL) honey
1 Tbsp (15 mL) butter
4 cups (1 L) chopped mushrooms (chanterelle, button, pine, etc.)
2 Tbsp (30 mL) chopped fresh dill
Salt and pepper, to taste
1 Tbsp (15 mL) rosehip butter (or rosehip syrup or apple butter)
1 Tbsp (15 mL) mustard (yellow or grainy)
2 Tbsp (30 mL) grapeseed oil

1. Heat a large pot of boiling salted water. Cook the cauliflower until tender and then drain. Return the cauliflower to the pot and while it is still hot, add 2 tablespoons (30 mL) of the cider vinegar and the honey. Toss to mix. In a skillet over medium-high heat, add the butter. When it is sizzling, add the mushrooms and sauté until they begin to brown. Add the mushrooms to the cauliflower and toss to coat. Season well with dill, salt, and pepper.
2. In a small bowl, combine the rosehip butter, remaining 1 tablespoon (15 mL) of cider vinegar, and mustard. Whisk until smooth, then add the oil in a slow stream while whisking until thick. To serve, arrange the salad on a platter and drizzle with the vinaigrette. Serve at room temperature or chilled.

MARINATED FLANK STEAK AND MUSHROOMS OVER THAI SALAD

SERVES 4

Make sure to cook the meat medium-rare and allow the steak to rest for at least as long as you cooked it. You can substitute red Thai curry paste for the marinade—it is available in most grocery stores. Meatier mushrooms like chanterelles, shiitakes, and shimeji are good choices for this recipe. Enoki mushrooms make a good garnish.

Marinated flank steak

1 lb (450 g) flank steak, trimmed
8 large shiitake mushroom caps
1 Tbsp (15 mL) minced fresh ginger
1 Tbsp (15 mL) minced garlic
1 tsp (5 mL) lime zest (or shredded fresh or dried kaffir lime leaves)
1 Tbsp (15 mL) chopped basil (preferably Thai basil)
1 Tbsp (15 mL) hot sauce
1 Tbsp (15 mL) fish sauce
2 Tbsp (30 mL) grapeseed oil

Thai salad

Zest and juice of 1 lime
1 Tbsp (15 mL) brown sugar
2 Tbsp (30 mL) fish sauce
¼ cup (60 mL) chopped mint (or basil or cilantro)
1 chili pepper, minced (jalapeno, serrano, or bird's eye)
2 Tbsp (30 mL) grapeseed oil
4 cups (1 L) shredded romaine lettuce
1 cup (250 mL) fresh bean sprouts
1 carrot, peeled and grated
Lime wedges, for garnish
Basil leaves, for garnish

1. Score the flank steak with a sharp knife. Place in a glass casserole dish and add the mushroom caps, ginger, garlic, lime zest, basil, hot sauce, fish sauce, and oil. Toss well to coat and let marinate for 15 minutes.
2. Prepare the dressing by placing the lime juice and zest, sugar, fish sauce, mint, and chili in a large salad bowl. Drizzle in the oil, whisking constantly, until smooth and thick. Set aside. Preheat the grill to high (400°F [200°C]).
3. Cook the flank steak over the grill for 5 minutes per side. Keep the steak rare. Grill the marinated mushrooms until soft and slightly charred. Remove the steak and mushrooms from the grill and let rest in a warm place for at least 5 minutes.
4. Add the lettuce, bean sprouts, and carrot to the dressing, tossing well to coat. Carve the beef and mushrooms into very thin slices and place on top of the salad. Garnish with lime wedges and basil leaves. Serve immediately.

SALAD OF PORCINI, TOMATOES, AND SALAMI WITH BLUE CHEESE DRESSING

SERVES 4–6

This salad is a special treat if you have fresh porcini mushrooms; however, you can also use chanterelles, hedgehogs, oysters, or portobello mushrooms. Use a good-quality salami, locally made if you can find it. Works well with salami flavoured with fennel seed or orange zest. Use the best tomatoes you can find. An assortment of red, yellow, and green heirloom tomatoes will be beautiful with the porcini.

2 Tbsp (30 mL) mayonnaise
1 Tbsp (15 mL) sherry vinegar
2 Tbsp (30 mL) crumbled local blue cheese (Stilton or Roquefort style)
1 Tbsp (15 mL) minced fresh chives (or green onion)
Freshly ground pepper, to taste
1 Tbsp (15 mL) olive oil
1 medium porcini, sliced
1 Tbsp (15 mL) minced garlic
Salt and pepper, to taste
12 thin slices salami (about 4 oz [115 g])
4 tomatoes, sliced (or 1 cup [250 mL] cherry tomatoes)

1. In a small bowl, combine the mayonnaise and vinegar. Whisk until smooth. Add the crumbled cheese and stir to mix. Adjust the consistency with water if needed to make a pourable sauce. Add the chives and season with freshly ground pepper.
2. In a sauté pan over medium-high heat, add the olive oil. When hot, add the mushroom and garlic. Sauté until the mushroom softens and begins to brown. Season well with salt and pepper.
3. Cut the salami slices into thin strips. To serve, place the tomato slices on a serving platter, seasoning well with salt and pepper. Top with the sautéed mushrooms and drizzle with the blue cheese dressing. Scatter the salami strips around the plate.

SALAD OF WILD MUSHROOMS, FENNEL, AND BRESAOLA

SERVES 4

Bresaola is salted and dried beef that has been aged for several months. Buy it from a good deli and have it sliced as thinly as possible. Cecina is the Spanish version and Bündnerfleisch is a German rendition, which is occasionally made in a smoked form. This recipe is great with chanterelles, hedgehogs, or porcini mushrooms. Use your best extra virgin olive oil for this recipe.

1 large fennel bulb, trimmed of browned outer leaves and stalk
1 Tbsp (15 mL) lemon juice
1 apple, preferably Fuji or Gala
1 Tbsp (15 mL) olive oil
2 cups (500 mL) sliced mushrooms (chanterelle, porcini, button, etc.)
1 Tbsp (15 mL) minced garlic
1 small red onion, very thinly sliced
Salt and pepper, to taste
4 oz (115 g) thinly sliced bresaola (or cecina or Bündnerfleisch)
Good olive oil, for drizzling
Parmesan cheese wedge, for garnish

1. Cut the hard white base off the fennel bulb. With a sharp knife or mandoline, cut the fennel into thin rounds. Toss with the lemon juice. Quarter the apple and remove the core. Slice thinly and add to the fennel and set aside.
2. In a sauté pan over medium-high heat, add the olive oil, mushrooms, and garlic. Sauté until the mushrooms give off moisture and begin to brown. Add the onion at the end and toss to warm through (keep it fairly firm). Add to the fennel mix, seasoning well with salt and pepper and tossing to combine.
3. Mound the fennel salad onto a serving plate. Place the bresaola on top of the salad. Drizzle the salad and around the plate with good olive oil. Shave chunks of Parmesan with a vegetable peeler and place it around the plate. Season with a grinding of fresh pepper. Serve with good crusty bread or crackers.

ROASTED MUSHROOM FATTOUSH SALAD

SERVES 4

A great salad with Middle Eastern roots made here with toasted pita bread and a variety of vegetables and mushrooms. Buy a good selection of olives and remove the pits by flattening the olive with the side of a chef's knife. I like kalamata (black) and picholine (green) olives mixed together.

2 cups (500 mL) sliced mushrooms (chanterelle, button, oyster, etc.)
2 Tbsp (30 mL) olive oil
2 Tbsp (30 mL) chopped garlic
Salt and pepper, to taste
4 pita breads, cut into thin wedges
1 cup (250 mL) seeded and diced cucumber
1 red pepper, seeded and cubed
2 fresh ripe tomatoes, chopped
¼ cup (60 mL) crumbled feta cheese
½ cup (125 mL) pitted olives
Juice of 1 lemon
2 Tbsp (30 mL) olive oil
2 Tbsp (30 mL) chopped fresh parsley
1 tsp (5 mL) sumac powder (optional)

1. Preheat the oven to 350°F (180°C).
2. Spread the mushrooms on a baking tray and drizzle with olive oil and garlic. Season them well with salt and pepper and place in the oven. Roast for 10 minutes, then distribute the pita wedges on top of the mushrooms. Roast for a further 5 minutes, or until the pita is crispy and beginning to brown. Remove from the oven and let cool to room temperature.
3. In a salad bowl, combine the cucumber, red pepper, tomatoes, feta cheese, and olives. Add the lemon juice and olive oil. Season with salt and pepper and then add the mushroom and pita mixture to the bowl. Toss well to mix and adjust seasoning if needed. Just before serving, add the chopped parsley on top and sprinkle with the sumac powder (if using). Serve at room temperature.

SALAD OF GRILLED RADICCHIO, MUSHROOMS, AND SARDINES WITH MUSHROOM AÏOLI

SERVES 4

An easy recipe for the summer barbecue season. Whole sardines are available fresh in the spring and frozen the rest of the year. The oily fish is a good source of omega-3 fatty acids and a great source of vitamin B2. These nutrients help boost your metabolism and are important for heart health. Portobello mushrooms are a good choice for this dish.

---

1 recipe mushroom aïoli (p. 96)
2 small radicchio heads
2 cups (500 mL) mushrooms, whole or cut into thick slices (portobello, porcini, chanterelle, porcini, oyster, etc.)
8 sardines, cleaned
2 Tbsp (30 mL) olive oil
1 Tbsp (15 mL) minced garlic
2 Tbsp (30 mL) chopped fresh basil
Salt and pepper, to taste

---

1. Preheat the barbecue to high.
2. Make the mushroom aïoli according to the directions. Keep chilled until needed.
3. Trim the ends off the radicchio heads. Cut into thick wedges, leaving the stems attached. Place on a baking tray and add the mushrooms and sardines. Drizzle with olive oil, garlic, and basil. Season well with salt and pepper. Toss to coat.
4. Place the radicchio, mushrooms, and sardines directly on the grill. Cook until browned, about 3–4 minutes per side. Transfer to a serving platter. Drizzle with the aïoli and serve immediately.

SEAFOOD

SWEDISH MUSHROOM AND CRAB PANCAKES

MAKES 8–10 PANCAKES

These pancakes are like crepes but made with more egg to give them a softer texture. Use a non-stick sauté pan or well-seasoned steel crepe pan to make them. They can be made well in advance and assembled just before serving.

Pancakes
4 eggs
2 cups (500 mL) milk
½ cup (125 mL) all-purpose flour
Pinch of salt and pepper
2 Tbsp (30 mL) melted butter

Filling
1 Tbsp (15 mL) salted butter
1 onion, peeled and diced
4 cups (1 L) chopped mushrooms (chanterelle, button, pine, etc.)
1 cup (250 mL) sour cream (or cream cheese)
1 cup (250 mL) Dungeness crabmeat
2 Tbsp (30 mL) fresh fennel fronds (or fresh dill, chopped, or 1 Tbsp [15 mL] fresh tarragon)
Salt and pepper, to taste
Melted butter, for brushing

1. In a large bowl, beat the eggs with a wire whisk. Mix in the milk, flour, salt, pepper, and melted butter. Let stand for at least 20 minutes.
2. Warm a non-stick skillet over medium heat. Pour a thin layer of the batter into the skillet and swirl the pan to spread the batter to the edges. Cook until the top surface appears dry. Flip with a spatula and cook for another 2 minutes, or until golden brown. Place on a platter and set aside. Repeat until no more batter remains.
3. In a skillet over medium-high heat, add the butter. When sizzling, add the onion and mushrooms and sauté until they begin to release moisture. Continue cooking until the mushrooms and onion begin to brown. Add to a mixing bowl, along with the sour cream, crabmeat, and fennel. Season with salt and pepper.
4. Preheat the oven to 350°F (180°C).
5. To serve, place a pancake on a clean surface. Place a little filling along the edge of the pancake. Roll up into a tight log and place in a casserole dish. Repeat with remaining pancakes and filling. Brush each log with melted butter and place in the oven for 10 minutes, or until just warmed through. Serve immediately.

HALIBUT, MOREL, AND LEEK PHYLLO ROLL

SERVES 4

Use the whites of the leeks for this recipe. Leave some of the lighter green but chop off all the deep green. Slice off the bottom root ends, cut the leeks in half, and soak in cold water until needed. You can buy the halibut in one slab and cut into 1-inch (2.5 cm) slices. This dish is best made just before serving as the phyllo will soften as it cools and sits. Excellent with a little tomato mushroom sauce (p. 222) spooned on the plate.

2 Tbsp (30 mL) butter
4 leeks, trimmed and washed
1 Tbsp (15 mL) minced garlic
1 oz (28 g) morels, soaked and then chopped into rings
1 cup (250 mL) whipping cream
1 Tbsp (15 mL) minced parsley or chives
Salt and pepper, to taste
8 sheets phyllo pastry
2 Tbsp (30 mL) melted butter
4 pieces halibut fillet (about 4 oz [115 g] each)

1. In a skillet over medium-high heat, add the butter and heat until sizzling. Add the leeks, garlic, and morels. Sauté until the leeks soften and begin to brown. Add the whipping cream and parsley and bring to a boil. Reduce until the mixture thickens. Season well with salt and pepper. Let cool completely.
2. Place a phyllo sheet on a clean work surface. Brush with melted butter and top with a second sheet. Cut the 2 sheets into 4 quarters. Lay a thin line of the morel mixture along one side of the sheet, keeping around 1 inch (2.5 cm) free of filling at each end.
3. Top with a halibut slice and fold phyllo overtop of the filling. Fold each end of the roll overtop of the pastry. Continue rolling the filling into a tight roll. Brush the last edge with a little butter and fold to seal tightly. Place on a tray covered with parchment paper. Repeat with remaining filling and phyllo. Refrigerate until needed.
4. Preheat the oven to 375°F (190°C).
5. Brush chilled rolls with a little melted butter and place in the oven. Bake for 10–12 minutes, or until the pastry is browned and crisp. Transfer to serving plates and serve warm.

GRILLED SALMON WITH BACON MUSHROOM JAM

SERVES 4

Everything seems to go better with bacon and this combination keeps proving that theory. This jam is actually more of a sweet and sour effort with the addition of lemon juice and zest to cut the sweetness and fat. This combination is also great with scallops and prawns. The salmon dressing will cause the surface to char quickly so keep an eye on the fish as you grill it. You can also cook the salmon on a cedar plank with great results.

Bacon mushroom jam
4 slices thick-cut bacon, diced
2 cups (500 mL) diced assorted mushrooms (button, chanterelle, porcini, etc.)
1 Tbsp (15 mL) chopped garlic
3 Tbsp (45 mL) honey
Zest and juice of 1 lemon
1 tsp (5 mL) hot sauce
Salt and pepper, to taste

Salmon
1 tsp (5 mL) honey (or maple syrup)
1 Tbsp (15 mL) soy sauce
1 Tbsp (15 mL) mustard
1 tsp (5 mL) sesame oil
4 wild salmon fillets (about 6 oz [180 g] each)
2 Tbsp (30 mL) sesame seeds, for garnish
Lemon wedges

1. In a skillet over medium-high heat, add the bacon and begin to render the fat. Add the mushrooms and garlic. Sauté until the mushrooms soften and begin to brown. Add the honey and melt it into the mushrooms. Add the lemon zest and juice and the hot sauce. Taste and adjust with salt and pepper, if necessary. Set aside to cool slightly.
2. In a small bowl, combine the honey, soy sauce, mustard, and sesame oil. Stir to mix. Place the salmon on a plate and drizzle the dressing overtop. Flip the salmon to coat in the dressing. Let stand for 10 minutes while you heat a barbecue to high.
3. Clean and oil the grill. Place the salmon on the grill and cook for about 3–4 minutes per side, or until the salmon just begins to char. Transfer to a serving platter. Top with the bacon mushroom jam, sprinkle with sesame seeds, and serve with lemon wedges.

MANILA CLAMS WITH PORCINI AND CHORIZO

SERVES 4

This dish is all about the flavours of Portugal and Spain. Try to find some sherry vinegar to bring the dish to another level. This dish is amazing with porcini mushrooms but is also excellent with chanterelles or morels. Serve with slices of crusty bread.

3 Tbsp (45 mL) olive oil
¼ cup (60 mL) finely chopped chorizo sausage
1 small onion, peeled and minced
1 cup (250 mL) diced porcini mushrooms
2 Tbsp (30 mL) sherry vinegar
2 lb (1 kg) Manila clams
¼ cup (60 mL) dry white wine
1 Tbsp (15 mL) minced garlic
1 Tbsp (15 mL) minced flat-leaf parsley, for garnish

1. In a skillet, add the olive oil, chorizo, onion, and mushrooms. Heat over medium-high until the chorizo begins to cook and the mushrooms begin to brown. Add the sherry vinegar and stir to mix. Set aside but keep warm.
2. In a large, heavy-bottomed pot over high heat, bring the clams, wine, and garlic to a boil. Cover with a lid, cooking for 2–3 minutes, or until the majority of the clams begin to open. Large clams might take a little longer. As the clams open, you can remove them and transfer to a bowl. When all of the clams are open, transfer to a serving bowl and top with the chorizo and mushroom mixture and garnish with the flat-leaf parsley. Serve warm.

POACHED LING COD WITH ROASTED WILD MUSHROOMS, TOMATOES, AND GARLIC

SERVES 4

Use the best tomatoes you can find for this dish. Out of season try some hothouse cherry tomatoes and reduce the cooking time to 20 minutes. You can also use any combination of cultivated mushrooms, particularly shimeji and oyster mushrooms.

4 medium tomatoes, quartered
2 cups (500 mL) chanterelles (or fairy rings, winter chanterelles, etc.)
1 garlic bulb, separated into peeled cloves
2 Tbsp (30 mL) shredded fresh basil leaves
1 tsp (5 mL) sea salt
1 tsp (5 mL) hot sauce
¼ cup (60 mL) olive oil
1 cup (250 mL) dry white wine
1 tsp (5 mL) minced fresh thyme
1 bay leaf
4 fillets ling cod or Pacific cod (about 6 oz [180 g] each)

1. Preheat the oven to 350°F (180°C).
2. In a cast-iron skillet (or roasting pan), add the tomatoes, chanterelles, garlic cloves, basil, sea salt, and hot sauce. Drizzle the olive oil overtop and place in the oven to roast for 30 minutes. Remove from the oven and let rest for 30 minutes. (Can be made in advance and reheated before serving—remove the skins from the tomatoes before reheating; they should slip off easily.)
3. In a small ovenproof skillet over medium heat, bring the wine, thyme, and bay leaf to a boil. Reduce the heat and add the ling cod. Poach for about 7 minutes. Gently transfer the fish to a plate and set aside. Reduce the wine down to a few tablespoons. Add the roasted tomato mixture and reheat. Return the cod pieces to the pan and reheat to warm through. Serve warm with potatoes or rice.

PAN-SEARED SCALLOPS AND JAPANESE-STYLE MUSHROOMS

SERVES 4–6

Sweet scallops are a nice match for the acidity of these lightly pickled mushrooms. Almost any mushroom will work in this pickle recipe, particularly Japanese varieties like shimeji, maitake, or nameko mushrooms.

---

3 Tbsp (45 mL) grapeseed oil, divided
2 cups (500 mL) mushrooms, whole or cut in thick slices
(shiitake, oyster, chanterelle, porcini, button, etc.)
1 Tbsp (15 mL) orange marmalade
1 Tbsp (15 mL) pickled ginger
½ cup (125 mL) rice wine vinegar
1 Tbsp (15 mL) light soy sauce
Salt and pepper, to taste
1 lb (450 g) scallops
Toasted sesame seeds, for garnish

---

1. In a non-stick skillet, add 1 tablespoon (15 mL) of the grapeseed oil and sauté the mushrooms until they just start to brown. Add the marmalade, pickled ginger, rice wine vinegar, and soy sauce. Season with salt and pepper. Remove from the pan and let cool. Refrigerate until needed.
2. Warm 2 tablespoons (30 mL) of the oil in a non-stick sauté pan over medium-high heat. Pat the scallops with a paper towel and add to the pan. Sear each scallop until golden brown and transfer to a warm plate. To serve, mound a pile of mushrooms on the plate and top with the scallops. Sprinkle with some sesame seeds and serve immediately.

GRILLED OYSTERS WITH PORCINI AND GOAT CHEESE

SERVES 4

Beach oysters are large, mature oysters that are sold for grilling on the barbecue. You can substitute shucked oysters that are available in tubs. Poach the shucked oysters in their juice for 2 minutes first and then transfer to a gratin dish. This dish also works well with truffle paste added to the béchamel. Serve with slices of baguette or crusty bread.

1 recipe porcini béchamel sauce (p. 224)
12 large beach oysters
½ cup (125 mL) crumbled soft goat cheese
1 Tbsp (15 mL) minced fresh chives

1. Preheat a barbecue to high.
2. Prepare the béchamel according to the directions. Place whole oysters on the barbecue and heat until they pop open. Transfer to a baking tray and open. Use a towel to shield your hands from the heat and from any shards of oyster shell.
3. Add 2 spoonfuls of béchamel to each oyster shell and top with the goat cheese and chives. Return to the barbecue and close the lid. Cook oysters for 5 minutes, or until the sauce is warmed through and bubbles. The goat cheese may not melt but will be warm. Oysters can be placed under a broiler to brown, if desired. Serve hot with bread to scoop the sauce and oysters onto.

MUSSELS WITH CHANTERELLES, TOMATOES, AND ROSEMARY

SERVES 4

These mussels remind me of the flavours of the Mediterranean. Chanterelles are excellent in tomato sauce, but you can also use cauliflower fungi, oyster mushrooms, or pine mushrooms. Fresh mussels should have no odour but will smell like the sea. Strong aromas indicate the mussels are not fresh. A fresh mussel will also be tightly closed. Discard any that are open before cooking and any that do not open during cooking. Cook until the mussels just open and are still tender and plump.

---

2 Tbsp (30 mL) olive oil
1 Tbsp (15 mL) minced garlic
1 cup (250 mL) finely sliced chanterelle mushrooms
1 large tomato, cored and diced
½ cup (125 mL) dry white wine
1 Tbsp (15 mL) chopped fresh rosemary
2 lb (1 kg) mussels
2 Tbsp (30 mL) salted butter, cut into cubes
Green onion, minced, for garnish

---

1. Heat a large sauté pan over medium-high. Add the olive oil and garlic. Add the chanterelles and sauté until the mushrooms give off moisture and begin to brown. Add the tomato, wine, and rosemary. Bring to a boil and then toss in the mussels.
2. Cover and steam for 5 minutes, or until the mussels open. Stir to gently mix the mussels and make sure they all have a chance to heat and open. Add the butter and gently shake the pan to incorporate into the sauce. Garnish with minced green onion and serve warm with fresh, sliced baguette.

SAUCES FOR PASTA, RICE, AND GNOCCHI

TOMATO MUSHROOM SAUCE

MAKES ABOUT 10 CUPS (2.5 L)

This sauce is one of my all-time favourite ways to preserve the wild mushroom harvest. It is particularly good with chanterelles, but I have also had excellent results with pine mushrooms, cauliflower fungi, and hedgehog mushrooms. If you are not so lucky, the sauce is also great with almost every cultivated mushroom available.

2 Tbsp (30 mL) olive oil
1 large onion, chopped
1 Tbsp (15 mL) honey
1 whole garlic bulb, peeled and minced
2 celery stalks
2 cups (500 mL) sliced mushrooms
8 cups (2 L) stewed tomatoes
2 bay leaves
1 Tbsp (15 mL) chopped fresh rosemary
1 Tbsp (15 mL) chopped fresh sage
2 Tbsp (30 mL) chopped fresh basil
1 tsp (5 mL) hot sauce
Salt and pepper, to taste

1. In a large stockpot, add the olive oil and onion. Heat until the onion begins to brown, then add the honey and stir until the mixture starts to sizzle. Add the garlic, celery, and mushrooms, stirring until the mixture browns and just begins to stick to the bottom of the pan. Add the tomatoes and stir well to mix. Reduce the heat to a simmer and add the bay leaves, rosemary, sage, and basil. Stir to mix and then season with hot sauce, salt, and pepper.
2. Simmer for 1 hour, stirring occasionally. Purée with an immersion blender and then strain through a sieve into a storage container. The sauce can be refrigerated for 3–4 days or can be frozen for up to 1 month. Transfer to zip-lock bags and freeze flat on a cookie tray. When frozen, stack bags to store in the freezer.

PORCINI BÉCHAMEL SAUCE

MAKES ABOUT 2 CUPS (500 ML)

Béchamel is another mother sauce that can be used in a number of preparations. The sauce will thicken as it sits. Thin down with additional milk if necessary to achieve a pourable consistency. You can also make a wheat-free version using rice flour or tapioca flour.

2 Tbsp (30 mL) butter
2 Tbsp (30 mL) flour
1 Tbsp (15 mL) porcini powder (p. 73)
2 cups (500 mL) milk (or half milk and half stock)
Salt and pepper, to taste

1. In a saucepan over medium-high heat, add the butter. Heat until sizzling, then add the flour and whisk until smooth. Add the porcini powder and stir to mix. Add the milk and whisk until smooth. Cook for 10 minutes over low heat until smooth and thick. Season well with salt and pepper. Serve as a sauce for pasta or vegetables, or use as the base in several recipes in this book.

PORCINI MORNAY SAUCE

MAKES ABOUT 2 CUPS (500 ML)

This sauce can be modified by whatever cheese you add to the mix. White cheddar is sharp and smooth, goat cheese will make the sauce tangy, and blue cheese will give you a sharp and strongly flavoured sauce that will add punch to whatever you pair it with. This sauce is particularly good when paired with a neutral vegetable like steamed cauliflower. Use any leftover sauce to make the mushroom croque monsieur (p. 146).

1 recipe porcini béchamel sauce (p. 224)
1 cup (250 mL) shredded cheese
1 Tbsp (15 mL) minced fresh mild herbs (chives, parsley, marjoram, etc.)

1. Prepare the béchamel sauce according to directions. Stir in the cheese and herbs. Check the seasoning and adjust with salt and pepper. Keep warm until needed.

BRAISED LEEKS IN MUSHROOM HERB SAUCE

MAKES ABOUT 3 CUPS (750 ML)

This sauce is excellent with gnocchi or gnudi. The sauce can be thickened with rice flour or tapioca or cornstarch. You can adjust the thickness by changing the amount of starch you add to the liquid. The sauce can be finished with a tablespoon (15 mL) of butter or cream to add more richness.

1 Tbsp (15 mL) olive oil
1 Tbsp (15 mL) minced garlic
6 leeks, trimmed, washed, and sliced
2 cups (500 mL) sliced mushrooms (morel, button, oyster, etc.)
1 tsp (5 mL) honey
¼ cup (60 mL) dry white wine
2 cups (500 mL) chicken stock (or vegetable stock or water)
1 Tbsp (15 mL) rice flour
Salt and pepper, to taste
2 Tbsp (30 mL) herbs (flat-leaf parsley, thyme, sage, etc.)

1. In a skillet, add the olive oil and garlic. When it begins to sizzle, add the leeks and mushrooms. Sauté until the leeks wilt and begin to brown. Add the honey and let melt and begin to caramelize. Add the wine and reduce until it has all evaporated. Add the stock and bring to a boil. Cook for 5 minutes. Mix the rice flour with 1 tablespoon (15 mL) cold water. Add this slurry to the pan and stir until sauce thickens. Adjust with more stock or water, if needed, to make a nice sauce consistency. Season with salt and pepper. Garnish with fresh herbs and serve immediately.

MORELS IN MUSTARD CREAM

MAKES ABOUT 4 SERVINGS

This sauce is excellent over your favourite noodles. I like it over spaghettini or with penne or rotini. It is also wonderful with gnocchi or other dumplings.

2 oz (60 g) dried morels, presoaked in water
2 Tbsp (30 mL) salted butter
1 medium onion, minced
1 Tbsp (15 mL) minced garlic
2 Tbsp (30 mL) grainy mustard
1 cup (250 mL) chicken or mushroom stock
¼ cup (60 mL) whipping cream (optional)
3 Tbsp (45 mL) minced fresh chives
Salt and pepper, to taste

1. Remove the morels from the liquid and chop into rings. Transfer 1 cup (250 mL) of the soaking liquid to a clean container, leaving behind the bottom third of the liquid (and any sediment). Return the morels to the clean liquid and set aside.
2. In a saucepan over medium-high, heat the butter, onion, and garlic. Sauté the onion until it softens and begins to brown. Add the morels and soaking liquid to the pan. Add the mustard and stock. Bring to a boil and reduce the volume by about half. Add the whipping cream (if using) and stir well to mix. Reduce until the mixture reaches a sauce consistency (it will coat the back of a spoon). Add the chives and adjust seasoning with salt and pepper.

MUSHROOM AND CHARRED BROCCOLI SAUCE

MAKES ABOUT 4 PORTIONS

A versatile sauce that is great as a pasta sauce or equally tasty as a sauce for chicken or pork chops. This is a good sauce to use with mushrooms that have a soft texture, such as cauliflower fungi, winter chanterelles, or fairy ring mushrooms.

1 Tbsp (15 mL) olive oil
1 lb (450 g) broccoli florets
1 onion, diced
1–2 garlic cloves, minced
2 cups (500 mL) sliced mushrooms (button, chanterelle, cauliflower, etc.)
2 cups (500 mL) chicken stock
1 Tbsp (15 mL) salted butter (optional)
2 Tbsp (30 mL) freshly shredded Parmesan cheese

1. In a skillet over medium-high heat, add the olive oil and broccoli. Sauté until the broccoli starts to brown and crisp up. Add the onion, garlic, and mushrooms and sauté until the onion begins to soften and the mushrooms begin to colour. Add the chicken stock, turn the heat to high, and cook, stirring occasionally, until the broccoli is cooked through and the stock begins to reduce in volume (by about half). Add the butter and Parmesan cheese. Toss well and serve warm.

HUNTER-STYLE CHICKEN AND CHANTERELLE SAUCE

SERVES 4

The potato starch forms a crust on the chicken and keeps it very soft and moist. This is a great sauce for gnocchi or served over fresh or dried pasta. You can used a dried salami instead of the bacon with excellent results.

2 medium chicken breasts, skin removed
½ cup (125 mL) potato starch (or all-purpose flour)
1 Tbsp (15 mL) porcini powder (p. 73)
Salt and pepper, to taste
2 Tbsp (30 mL) olive oil
2 slices thick-cut bacon, cut into thick strips
1 small onion, peeled and diced
1 Tbsp (15 mL) minced garlic
1 Tbsp (15 mL) minced fresh rosemary
2 cups (500 mL) mushrooms (chanterelle, pine, button, shiitake, etc.)
½ cup (125 mL) red wine
2 cups (500 mL) chicken stock
2 Tbsp (30 mL) tomato paste

1. Place the chicken on a cutting board and cut into thin slices. Next, cut each slice into strips or chunks. Place in a small mixing bowl and add the starch and porcini powder. Season well with salt and pepper, then toss to coat.
2. Warm a skillet over medium-high heat and add the olive oil and chicken. Toss the pieces to break them up and then let the chicken cook for about 2 minutes undisturbed. Flip the chicken over to cook the other side of the strips for an additional 2 minutes. Remove the chicken and transfer to a clean bowl—do not worry if it is not cooked through. Drain the fat and add the bacon, onion, garlic, rosemary, and mushrooms to the pan. Sauté until the onion and mushrooms soften and begin to brown. Add the red wine and cook until reduced by half. Add the stock and tomato paste and stir to mix.
3. Return the chicken to the pan, taking care to leave any fat behind. Reduce the sauce until it thickens and the chicken is cooked through, about 5 minutes. Taste and adjust seasoning. Serve hot over gnocchi or pasta.

MUSHROOM PESTO

MAKES ABOUT 2 CUPS (500 ML)

This technique is similar to a French preparation called duxelles. Cooked mushrooms are puréed with herbs, garlic, and butter (or olive oil). The resulting paste can be frozen and used to instantly pump flavour into a sauce or soup. I freeze the pesto in an old ice cube tray and then place the cubes in a zip-lock bag so they are ready for quick use. I like to use chanterelles because they are plentiful, but it is really excellent with softer mushrooms like shaggy parasols or shaggy manes.

2 Tbsp (30 mL) butter (or olive oil)
1 cup (250 mL) minced onions
1 Tbsp (15 mL) minced garlic
4 cups (1 L) sliced shaggy parasol mushrooms (or chanterelle or button mushrooms)
1 Tbsp (15 mL) minced fresh sage
1 Tbsp (15 mL) minced fresh thyme
1 Tbsp (15 mL) minced fresh rosemary
Salt and pepper, to taste
Olive oil, for blending

1. Warm a sauté pan over medium-high heat and add the butter, onions, and garlic. Sauté until the onions soften, about 1–2 minutes. Add the mushrooms and toss to coat. Sauté until the mushrooms soften and begin to brown. Add the sage, thyme, and rosemary. Toss to warm to warm through. Season with salt and pepper.
2. Transfer to a food processor and pulse into a paste. With the machine running, add enough olive oil to make a smooth and soft purée. Transfer to a storage container. Can be kept in the fridge for 1 week or frozen for up to 2 months.

MUSHROOM PESTO CREAM

SERVES 4

A quick sauce that makes a great topping for pasta, chicken, fish, or shellfish. Try it spooned onto grilled beach oysters cooked on the barbecue. If you are making this sauce from frozen cubes of mushroom pesto (freeze in an ice cube tray for up to 3 months), it will take two large cubes to flavour 1 cup (250 mL) of cream.

¼ cup (60 mL) mushroom pesto
1 cup (250 mL) whipping cream
Salt and pepper, to taste

1. In a sauté pan over medium-high heat, add the mushroom pesto and whipping cream. Reduce until the sauce coats the back of a spoon and then season with salt and pepper. To serve, toss with cooked pasta and freshly grated Parmesan cheese.

MEAT AND POULTRY

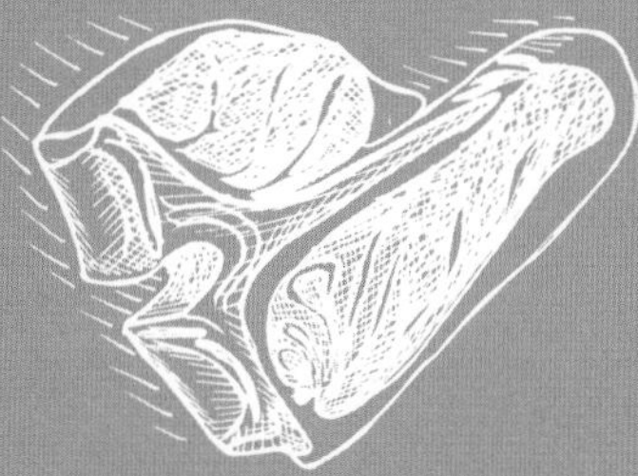

BRAISED RABBIT FROM RECIPE ON PAGE 242

BEEF MUSHROOM BURGER

MAKES 4 BURGERS

This might just be the ultimate burger for the mushroom lover—especially if you serve it with mushroom ketchup (p. 114). You can also use ground turkey with excellent results. The bread may seem like filler, but it makes the beef a little lighter in texture and adds flavour and fibre if you use a good crusty multi-grain loaf.

1 lb (450 g) ground beef
1 Tbsp (15 mL) porcini powder (p. 73)
2 cups (500 mL) diced button mushrooms
1 cup (250 mL) cubed multi-grain bread
1 small onion, finely diced
1 Tbsp (15 mL) Worcestershire sauce
1 Tbsp (15 mL) minced fresh rosemary
1 Tbsp (15 mL) minced garlic
1 tsp (5 mL) hot sauce

Garnish

4 slices good cheese (aged white cheddar, Edam, brie, etc.)
4 kaiser rolls or hamburger buns
Mushroom ketchup (p. 114)
Tomato slices
Pickles
Iceberg lettuce

1. In a mixing bowl, add the beef, porcini powder, button mushrooms, bread, onion, Worcestershire sauce, rosemary, garlic, and hot sauce. Mix with your hands until the mixture is smooth. Form into 4 patties and press to make uniform discs.
2. Heat the grill to hot and cook the burgers for about 5 minutes. Flip and top with the cheese. Grill with the lid closed for about 5 minutes. The burgers should be cooked through and the cheese melted. Toast the buns on the grill and brush with butter. Add the burgers and top with mushroom ketchup (or mushroom chutney, p. 112), tomato slices, pickles, and lettuce.

CHINESE BRAISED BEEF SHORT RIBS AND MUSHROOMS

SERVES 4

Ginger will help to tenderize the beef and make it meltingly tender. Use firm mushrooms that will stand up to the long cooking time. Dried mushrooms like porcini and morels also work very well in this dish.

¼ cup (60 mL) flour
1 tsp (5 mL) five-spice powder
Salt and pepper, to taste
3 lb (1.3 kg) beef short ribs
2 Tbsp (30 mL) olive oil
4 cups (1 L) beef stock (or beer or wine)
2 onions, peeled and sliced
1 celery stalk, sliced
4 cups (1 L) assorted mushrooms (shiitake, maitake, shimeji, button, etc.)
6 slices fresh ginger
2 Tbsp (30 mL) minced garlic
2 Tbsp (30 mL) hoisin sauce
1 Tbsp (15 mL) dark soy sauce
2 Tbsp (30 mL) tomato paste

1. Preheat the oven to 350°F (180°C).
2. In a small mixing bowl, combine the flour, five-spice powder, salt, and pepper. Stir to mix.
3. Add the ribs, one at a time, and coat with the flour mixture. Transfer to a hot skillet with the olive oil. Repeat with the remaining ribs. Turn frequently until all sides are browned. Reduce heat if they start to brown too quickly or smoke.
4. Transfer to a roasting pan and add the beef stock, onions, celery, mushrooms, ginger, garlic, hoisin sauce, soy sauce, and tomato paste. Cover tightly with aluminum foil and place in the oven for 2 hours. Remove from the oven and let cool for 1 hour. Transfer to a storage container and refrigerate overnight. The next day, remove any fat from the surface of the stock.
5. To serve, add the ribs and stock to a large skillet. Bring to a boil, then simmer, turning the meat occasionally while the stock reduces and the meat becomes very tender. You can leave the meat on the bone, or remove it and coarsely chop the flesh. Check the seasoning and adjust with salt and pepper, if necessary. Serve warm over steamed rice with steamed or sautéed Chinese vegetables (bok choy, gai lan, sui choy, etc.).

PAN-ROASTED, MUSHROOM-RUBBED RIB-EYE STEAK WITH PORCINI GRAVY

SERVES 2–4

We are lucky to have sources of grass-fed beef in our area. These amazing steaks should be sought out for their great beef flavour and healthy fats. If not available, look for an organic steak that has been dry aged by a good artisan butcher.

2 lb (1 kg) prime rib steak (at least 2 inches [5 cm] thick)
1 Tbsp (15 mL) minced garlic
1 Tbsp (15 mL) minced fresh rosemary
1 Tbsp (15 mL) porcini powder (p. 73)
Salt and pepper, to taste
1 Tbsp (15 mL) olive oil
1 Tbsp (15 mL) butter
1 large onion, peeled and diced
2 large carrots, peeled and chopped coarsely
2 celery stalks, chopped
¼ cup (60 mL) flour
1 Tbsp (15 mL) sweet sherry
4 cups (1 L) beef or mushroom stock
1 Tbsp (15 mL) butter
2 cups (500 mL) diced fresh porcini mushrooms (or button, portobello, chanterelle, morel, etc.)

1. Preheat the oven to 375°F (190°C).
2. Place the steak on a plate and sprinkle both sides with garlic, rosemary, and porcini powder. Season well with salt and pepper and drizzle with olive oil. Rub the seasoning into the meat. Allow the steak to rest for at least 10–15 minutes.
3. Place a cast-iron skillet over medium-high heat and add the olive oil and butter. Heat until sizzling and then add the meat, searing both sides until nicely browned, about 5 minutes per side. Add the onion, carrots, and celery to the pan, placing the beef on top of the vegetables. Transfer the pan to the oven and roast for at least 10 minutes (to an internal temperature of 145°F [63°C] for rare, 160°F [71°C] for medium, or 170°F [77°C] for well done).
4. Remove the pan from the oven and transfer the steak to a platter. Cover with aluminum foil and keep warm. Warm the skillet over medium heat until the vegetables brown and begin to stick to the bottom. Sprinkle the flour over the pan and stir to absorb any fat; lightly brown the flour. Add the sherry and stock, 1 cup (250 mL) at a time, until all the liquid is incorporated. The gravy will thicken as it simmers. Cook for 5 minutes, then pour through a strainer into a second pot, pressing any solids with a wooden spoon. Heat a skillet over medium-high and add the butter. Add the mushrooms and sauté until soft and beginning to brown. Add to the gravy and adjust seasoning with salt and pepper.
5. To serve, carve beef steak off the bone and cut into thick slices. Serve with mushroom gravy and porcini Yorkshire pudding (p. 100).

SLOW COOKER BARBECUE PULLED PORK AND MUSHROOMS

SERVES 6

A dish I like to cook on those slow winter days when the smell of the roasting pork will fill the house with the sweet promise of dinner. The pork is excellent on a bun topped with coleslaw. Look for locally raised pork for the best results.

3–4 lb (about 1.5 kg) pork shoulder roast
Salt and pepper
2 onions, sliced
2 cups (500 mL) minced button mushrooms
4 garlic cloves, minced
2 Tbsp (30 mL) minced fresh sage
2 Tbsp (30 mL) minced fresh rosemary
¼ cup (60 mL) tomato paste
1 cup (250 mL) tomato sauce
2 Tbsp (30 mL) molasses
¼ cup (60 mL) honey
½ cup (125 mL) apple cider vinegar
1 tsp (5 mL) hot sauce (or more to taste)
½ cup (125 mL) espresso (or strong coffee)

1. Rub the pork roast liberally with salt and pepper. Cover with plastic wrap and let stand for at least 30 minutes at room temperature. Meanwhile, in a saucepan, combine the onions, mushrooms, garlic, sage, rosemary, tomato paste, tomato sauce, molasses, honey, vinegar, hot sauce, and espresso. Bring to a simmer and stir well to mix.
2. Add the roast to a crockpot or slow cooker and pour the sauce overtop. (For extra flavour, you can brown the roast in a skillet beforehand.) Cover and cook on low heat for 8 hours. Gently transfer pork to a serving platter and cover with foil. Let rest for 20 minutes. Pour the remaining liquid into a large saucepan or measuring cup. Let settle and remove as much fat as possible from the surface. (If you are making this dish the day before serving, you can chill the sauce and then remove the fat.)
3. When the pork has cooled enough to handle, shred with two forks, removing any large chunks of fat or bone, if present. The mixture can be chilled and reheated up to 3 days later if desired. To serve, heat the sauce and bring to a boil. Add the shredded pork to a skillet and cover with the sauce. Toss to coat and warm through. Check the seasoning and add more salt and pepper, if needed. Serve warm on a bun with fresh coleslaw on the side.

WILD MUSHROOM PORCHETTA

SERVES 6–8

We are fortunate to be able to use beautiful artisan, heirloom pork. Try to find Black Berkshire (or Kurobuta) pork to make this an unforgettable meal. The cooking temperature of 145°F (63°C) will leave a slight pink blush to the meat, but it will be perfectly safe to eat, plus it will be moist and delicious.

2 Tbsp (30 mL) fennel seeds
1 Tbsp (15 mL) sea salt
2 tsp (10 mL) black peppercorns
1 tsp (5 mL) dried crushed chili flakes
1 Tbsp (15 mL) porcini powder (p. 73)
4 lb (about 2 kg) whole pork loin (or deboned shoulder), excess fat trimmed off with a thin layer left intact
2 Tbsp (30 mL) olive oil, plus additional for brushing
2 Tbsp (30 mL) minced garlic
2 Tbsp (30 mL) minced fresh rosemary
2 Tbsp (30 mL) minced fresh sage
1 lb (450 g) pancetta or bacon, sliced
2 cups (500 mL) chopped mushrooms (porcini, chanterelle, morel, etc.)

1. Prepare the rub by adding the fennel seeds to a skillet over medium-high. Heat until fragrant, then add salt, black peppercorns, and chili flakes. Toss to warm through and transfer to a bowl to cool. Powder in a spice grinder until medium fine. Add the porcini powder and mix. Set aside.
2. Place the pork in a glass casserole dish. Drizzle with olive oil and rub it over the surface of the meat. Rub the garlic, rosemary, and sage all the over the pork until evenly coated. Sprinkle with the spice rub mix and evenly coat. Cover with plastic wrap and refrigerate overnight.
3. Take 2 slices of pancetta or bacon and mince finely. In a sauté pan over medium-high heat, add the minced pancetta and the mushrooms. Sauté until the fat renders and the mushrooms begin to brown. Set aside and let cool. Make a long slit down the side of the loin, about halfway through the meat, and stuff the incision with the mushroom mixture.
4. Lay the remaining slices of pancetta on a cutting board. Place the pork loin overtop and wrap the bacon around the loin. Loop the pork with butcher twine and tie in a series of knots along the length of the roast.
5. Preheat one side of the barbecue to 350°F (180°C). Place the roast on a spit or on the unlit side of the barbecue for indirect heating (I used a smoker barbecue with a convection fan). Cover and barbecue for at least 1 hour and up to 2 hours, or to an internal temperature of 145°F (63°C). Let the pork rest for at least 15 minutes covered in aluminum foil. Remove the twine and cut into thin slices.

ROAST LEG OF LAMB STUFFED WITH PINE MUSHROOMS

SERVES 6–8

The herb mix used in this recipe is similar to Herbes de Provence, which is available as a dry mix in most grocery stores and is one of the few I would recommend if fresh herbs are not available to you.

1 whole leg of lamb, deboned (about 4 lb [2 kg])
1 Tbsp (15 mL) minced fresh sage
1 Tbsp (15 mL) minced fresh rosemary
1 tsp (5 mL) dried lavender (optional)
1 Tbsp (15 mL) minced fresh thyme leaves
1 Tbsp (15 mL) minced garlic
2 Tbsp (30 mL) olive oil
Salt and pepper, to taste
1 cup (250 mL) apple cider or dry white wine
1 cup (250 mL) minced pine mushrooms

1. Butterfly the leg of lamb by cutting it lengthwise to produce a fairly flat and spread out cut of meat. Try not to puncture the skin if possible. Sprinkle with sage, rosemary, lavender, thyme, garlic, and olive oil. Rub the mixture into the meat of the leg. Season well with salt and pepper. Flip the meat over so it is skin side up and pour the apple cider or wine overtop. Cover with plastic wrap and place in the fridge for at least 4 hours (overnight is better).
2. Preheat the oven to 400°F (200°C).
3. Remove the meat from the marinade and pat dry with paper towels. Sprinkle the pine mushrooms over the meat. Roll the leg into a long roll. Place the end of a roll of butcher twine under one end of the meat, twist the end of the twine under the other end, and pull tight to form a loop. Make a simple knot, loop the remaining end of twine in your hand, and slide it under the rolled lamb; repeat moving down the roast to make a tightly rolled bundle. (Alternately, you can cut smaller lengths of twine and tie them individually down the length of the roast.)
4. Season the skin very well with salt and pepper. Place the lamb in a roasting tray and put it into the oven. Roast for 45 minutes to 1 hour, or until a thermometer reads 130°F (54°C—for medium rare). Remove from the oven and cover with aluminum foil. Let rest for 10–15 minutes before removing the string and carving into slices. Serve warm with a reduction of lamb juices.

BRAISED RABBIT WITH MORELS, CABBAGE, AND BEER

SERVES 4–6

Prepare the rabbit by cutting off the leg and thigh. Separate into chunks. Cut the shoulders off the rabbit and cut into chunks. With a heavy knife, cut the rabbit up into 1-2 inch (2.5-5 cm) chunks. This dish can be made the day before and reheated before serving. While the meat is cool, you can also use the opportunity to remove all the bones and then just reheat the meat for a more elegant presentation.

1 rabbit, cut into chunks
1 Tbsp (15 mL) minced fresh sage
2 Tbsp (15 mL) minced garlic, divided
¼ cup (60 mL) flour
1 Tbsp (15 mL) morel powder (p. 73)
Salt and pepper, to taste
2 Tbsp (30 mL) olive oil
2 cups (500 mL) beer
2 cups (500 mL) chicken stock or water
1 Tbsp (15 mL) grainy mustard
2 cups (500 mL) fresh morels (or ½ cup [125 mL] dried), cut in quarters
2 onions, peeled and diced
2 cups (500 mL) finely shredded green cabbage

1. Place the rabbit in a casserole dish and season with sage and 1 tablespoon (15 mL) of the garlic. Set aside to marinate for at least 30 minutes. In a mixing bowl, combine the flour, morel powder, salt, and pepper.
2. Preheat the oven to 350°F (180°C).
3. Roll each piece of rabbit in the seasoned flour. Heat a sauté pan over medium-high and add the olive oil and rabbit in batches. Sauté until lightly browned. Transfer to a roasting pan and set aside until all the rabbit is browned. Don't worry if the meat is undercooked at this stage as it will cook completely in the second stage.
4. Add the beer, stock, remaining garlic, mustard, morels, onions, and cabbage to the roasting pan. Cover tightly with a lid (or aluminum foil) and place in the oven. Bake for 30–40 minutes and then remove from the oven. Serve over spaetzle, gnocchi, or buttered noodles.

CRISPY PORCINI FRIED CHICKEN

SERVES 4

A variation on a traditional fried chicken recipe, but taken to a new place with the addition of porcini powder and spices. The chicken is particularly delicious when drizzled with truffle honey. I use grapeseed oil for its high burning point.

1 whole chicken
2 onions, cut into thick rings
1 Tbsp (15 mL) minced garlic
4 cups (1 L) buttermilk
1 Tbsp (15 mL) hot sauce
2 cups (500 mL) flour
2 Tbsp (30 mL) porcini powder (p. 73)
1 tsp (5 mL) salt
1 tsp (5 mL) pepper
1 tsp (5 mL) ground coriander
1 tsp (5 mL) ground ginger
1 tsp (5 mL) cayenne pepper
4–6 cups (1–1.5 L) grapeseed oil

1. On a cutting board, place the bird breast side down. Cut off the wings at the second joint, leaving the wing drumettes attached. Cut off each leg and thigh and cut each into 2 pieces. Cut down the cavity of the chicken to free half the backbone. Peel back the spine to break it in half. Cut off the backbone with your knife and set aside. Continue working the knife downward to free the second half of the backbone. Place the chicken breast skin side down and cut in half along the breastbone, then cut each breast into 2 thick chunks.
2. Rinse chicken pieces under cold water and place in a mixing bowl. Add the onions, garlic, buttermilk, and hot sauce. Cover with plastic wrap and let stand for at least 2 hours.
3. In a casserole dish, combine the flour, porcini powder, salt, pepper, coriander, ginger, and cayenne pepper. Stir to mix. Take the chicken from the buttermilk and roll in the spiced flour. Place on a rack over a baking tray. Repeat with the remaining chicken. The onions can also be tossed in flour and fried.
4. Place enough oil in a pot to give you a depth of 3–4 inches (7.5–10 cm). Heat the oil to 365°F (185°C). Gently place the chicken in the oil and cook in batches to avoid overcrowding the pot. Cook for 7–8 minutes, or until the chicken is browned and very crispy. Transfer to a clean wire rack over a baking tray. Place in a warm oven and repeat with remaining chicken pieces. Let stand for 5 minutes and serve warm.

PAN-SEARED DUCK BREAST WITH PORCINI RAGOUT

SERVES 4

If you do not have access to porcini mushrooms you can use chanterelles, hedgehogs, or any cultivated mushroom. In place of the duck breast, you can use chicken breasts with excellent results.

4 duck breasts
Salt and pepper, to taste
1 onion, peeled and chopped
1 cup (250 mL) chopped porcini mushrooms
1 carrot, peeled and diced
1 celery stalk, trimmed and chopped
1 Tbsp (15 mL) chopped garlic
¼ cup (60 mL) flour
1 cup (250 mL) red wine
1 Tbsp (15 mL) minced fresh rosemary
4 cups (1 L) duck or mushroom stock

1. Place the duck flesh side down on a cutting board and trim the breasts of excess skin and side fat. Mince the excess fat finely and set it aside. With a sharp knife, make thin slashes about halfway into the fat diagonally and down the length of the breasts. Rotate the breasts 45 degrees and make slashes in the opposite direction. You will have little diamond cuts on the flesh when you are finished. Try not to cut into the flesh when you are cutting the fat. Season well with salt and pepper and set aside while you make the ragout.
2. Warm a saucepan over medium-high heat, then add the minced duck fat and crisp it while rendering the fat. Add the onion and sauté until lightly brown. Add the mushrooms, carrot, celery, and garlic. Sauté until the mixture just begins to brown. Sprinkle in the flour and stir to incorporate. Add the red wine and rosemary. Bring to a boil, scraping the bottom of the pan with a wooden spoon. Stir in the stock, reduce the heat to a simmer, and gently cook for 20 minutes. Adjust sauce with a little stock or water if it becomes too thick.
3. Meanwhile, preheat the oven to 350°F (180°C). Warm a sauté pan over medium-high heat, then add the breasts fat side down and cook until their skin is crispy and brown, about 7–8 minutes. There should be a lot of fat rendered in the pan. Reduce the heat if the skin starts to brown too quickly, or the pan begins to smoke.
4. Remove the breasts from the pan and place on a baking sheet, skin side up. Place in the oven and roast for 5 minutes. Remove from the oven and let rest for 15 minutes.
5. Ladle ragout on top of rice, potatoes, or buttered pasta. Slice the duck breast thinly and drape overtop of the ragout.

WHOLE ROASTED CHICKEN STUFFED WITH MUSHROOMS, CHESTNUTS, AND RICE

SERVES 4–6

A perfect dish for entertaining in the fall. The mushrooms, rice, and chestnuts make an addictive stuffing. The fresh herbs are also a key element, adding a beautiful herbal note to the rice. Make sure to check that the stuffing reaches an internal temperature of at least 165°F (74°C).

1 whole chicken (4 lb [2 kg])
1 Tbsp (15 mL) olive oil
1 Tbsp (15 mL) porcini powder (p. 73)
1 tsp (5 mL) cayenne powder
Salt and pepper, to taste
2 Tbsp (30 mL) butter
1 medium onion, peeled and diced
2 celery stalks, diced
2 Tbsp (30 mL) minced garlic
2 cups (500 mL) chopped mushrooms
1 cup (250 mL) chopped cooked chestnuts
1 Tbsp (15 mL) finely chopped fresh rosemary
1 Tbsp (15 mL) finely chopped fresh sage
2 Tbsp (30 mL) chopped fresh parsley
2 cups (500 mL) cooked short grain rice (white or brown)
2 cups (500 mL) apple cider (or water)

1. Remove the neck and giblets from the chicken if present. Rinse the chicken under cold water and pat dry with paper towels. Rub the chicken with olive oil, then sprinkle on the porcini powder, cayenne, salt, and pepper. Rub into the skin with your hands. Season the cavity well with salt and pepper and then set aside while you prepare the stuffing.
2. In a skillet over medium-high heat, add the butter and melt it. Add the onion, celery, and garlic. Sauté until the onion begins to brown, then add the mushrooms and heat until they release moisture and begin to brown. Remove the pan from the heat and empty contents into a mixing bowl to cool slightly. Add the chestnuts, rosemary, sage, parsley, and cooked rice. Stir to mix well and season with salt and pepper. Let cool to room temperature.
3. Preheat the oven to 375°F (190°C).
4. Place the chicken on a roasting pan and stuff with the rice mixture. If there is extra, stuff into the cavity at the neck of the chicken. Add the cider to the pan and then place the pan in the oven. Roast for 60–90 minutes, or until an internal temperature of 165°F (74°C) is reached. Remove from the oven and cover with aluminum foil. Let rest for at least 10 minutes before carving.

DESSERTS

LARGE CHANTERELLE

CHOCOLATE TRUFFLES^2

MAKES ABOUT 32

There is something poetic about chocolate truffles made with real truffles. They are delicious, no doubt about it, but also vaguely sensual and ultimately very pleasurable. In the words of the French philosopher Jean Anthelme Brillat-Savarin (1755–1826), "Whosoever says truffle utters a grand word, which awakens erotic and gastronomic ideas . . ." Add chocolate and you get truffles to the power of two.

8 oz (225 g) dark chocolate
⅔ cup (150 mL) whipping cream
1 tsp (5 mL) pure vanilla extract
1 tsp (5 mL) black truffle paste
¼ cup (60 mL) pure cocoa powder

1. On a cutting board, chop the chocolate into very fine shards. Place in a mixing bowl and set aside.
2. Place the cream in a saucepan and heat until boiling. Watch carefully as the cream can boil over very quickly. Pour the cream over the chocolate and stir to melt the chocolate. Add the vanilla extract and truffle paste. Let cool to room temperature. Cover with plastic wrap and chill for at least 2 hours.
3. With a small scoop or spoon, remove a small lump of chocolate and roll it into a ball. Work quickly as your hands will start to melt the chocolate. Place the ball on a tray and repeat with remaining chocolate. If it is warm, chill for 30 minutes. Roll each ball in cocoa and keep in an airtight container in the fridge. Serve chilled. Excellent with port or a fine red wine.

CARAMELIZED MUSHROOM GINGER UPSIDE-DOWN CAKE

MAKES 1 CAKE

Use the freshest mushrooms you can find for this cake. Choose firm, closed white button mushrooms. Wipe them clean and trim off any browned stems. Cut each mushroom into slices, then cut each slice into strips and the strips into dice. In spring, I like to put fresh Douglas fir tips into the cake batter for a delicious twist.

- 2 cups (500 mL) trimmed and diced button mushrooms
- ½ cup (125 mL) packed brown sugar
- ¼ cup (60 mL) minced candied ginger
- 3 Tbsp (45 mL) melted butter

Cake

- ½ cup (125 mL) butter, softened
- ¾ cup (180 mL) white sugar
- 2 eggs
- 2 tsp (10 mL) pure vanilla extract
- 1½ cups (375 mL) all-purpose flour
- 2 tsp (10 mL) baking powder
- ¼ tsp (1 mL) salt
- ⅛ tsp (0.5 mL) ground nutmeg
- 1 cup (250 mL) sour cream (or plain yogurt)

1. In a mixing bowl, combine the mushrooms, brown sugar, ginger, and melted butter. Stir to mix well and pour into the bottom of a non-stick loaf pan.
2. Preheat the oven to 350°F (180°C).
3. Using a mixer, cream together the butter and sugar until fluffy. Beat in the eggs one at a time, mixing well after each addition. Add the vanilla. Stir together the flour, baking powder, salt, and nutmeg. Fold in thirds into the creamed mixture alternating with sour cream, until all of the ingredients are just mixed.
4. Spread the batter over the mushroom mix. Bake in the oven for 45–50 minutes, or until the top springs back when pressed lightly. Let cool on a rack for 15 minutes. Run a knife around the edge of pan then invert the cake onto a serving plate. Serve warm or at room temperature. Best if eaten 1–2 days after baking but can be frozen for up to 1 month.

PINE MUSHROOM CRÈME CARAMEL

SERVES 6

Use the freshest pine mushrooms you can find for this dish. Young firm buttons are the most aromatic and will give you the most fragrant results. You can substitute the pine mushrooms for 1 teaspoon (5 mL) of truffle paste with excellent results.

1½ cups (375 mL) white sugar, divided
⅓ cup (85 mL) water
2 cups (500 mL) milk
¼ cup (60 mL) minced pine mushrooms
6 large eggs
1 tsp (5 mL) pure vanilla extract

1. In a heavy-bottomed saucepan (or skillet) over medium-high heat, combine 1 cup (250 mL) of the sugar and the water. Stir with a wooden spoon or a heatproof spatula until the sugar dissolves, about 2 minutes. Increase the heat to high and boil without stirring until the sugar caramelizes to a light golden brown. Swirl to distribute the caramel throughout the sugar mixture. Have 6 ramekin dishes ready in an ovenproof dish on a work surface near the stove. Quickly pour the caramel mixture evenly into the ramekins. Set aside until cool.
2. Preheat the oven to 325°F (160°C).
3. Add the milk and pine mushrooms to the caramel pan and stir to dissolve any remaining caramel. In a mixing bowl, add the remaining sugar and crack the eggs overtop. Whisk until well combined and the egg mixture lightens in colour. Bring the milk mixture to a boil, then quickly remove from the heat. Let the mixture sit for 5 minutes to infuse and cool slightly. Pour one-third of the milk into the egg mixture. Whisk to mix and pour the remaining milk overtop. Sieve the entire mixture into a bowl or serving jug (to remove any chunks of egg white that might have cooked). Stir in the vanilla extract.
4. Using a ladle (or pouring from the jug if used), divide the mixture among the ramekins, filling them but leaving a little room at the top.
5. Pour enough boiling water into the ovenproof dish to reach halfway up the sides of the ramekins. Top with the remaining egg mixture (if any remains). Place in the oven and bake 35–40 minutes, or until the custards are just set. When you jiggle the custard the outer edge should have started to firm up, while the centre will have a little more movement. Remove the dish from the oven and cool on a rack for 10 minutes. Remove ramekins from the pan and let cool to room temperature. Cover each with plastic wrap and refrigerate for at least 4 hours. To serve, run a knife around the edge of the ramekins and carefully turn onto serving plates. Jostle the ramekins until the custards slide out.

CANDIED CHANTERELLE PANNA COTTA

SERVES 8

Use small button chanterelles for the best results. They tend to have a firmer texture than other mushrooms, which adds a nice crunch to the candied mushrooms.

1 cup (250 mL) white sugar
1 cinnamon stick
2 cups (500 mL) thinly sliced button chanterelles
2 cups (500 mL) milk, divided
2 Tbsp (30 mL) gelatin powder (2 packages, or 6 sheets gelatin)
2¼ cups (560 mL) whipping cream, divided
1 vanilla bean (or 1 tsp [5 mL] vanilla extract)
¼ cup (60 mL) honey
Vegetable oil, for ramekins
Fresh berries or fruit, for garnish

1. In a saucepan, combine the sugar, 1 cup (250 mL) water, and the cinnamon stick. Bring to a boil and then add the chanterelles. Skim off any scum that forms on the surface. Reduce heat and simmer for 10 minutes. Remove from the stove, transfer to a glass jar, and let cool. Remove the cinnamon stick when you feel the flavours are extracted, or after about 15 minutes.
2. In a small saucepan, add 1 cup (250 mL) of the milk and the gelatin. Stir to dissolve and set aside for 5 minutes to steep and soften the gelatin.
3. In a large saucepan, combine 2 cups (500 mL) of the whipping cream, remaining milk, vanilla bean, and honey. Bring to a boil, then remove from heat immediately and add the gelatin mixture, stirring gently to mix. Test for sweetness and add more honey to taste (if desired). Strain panna cotta mixture into a bowl, removing the vanilla bean. Scrape the vanilla seeds into the mixture.
4. Rub 8 custard ramekins with a little oil, which helps to release the end result. Drain the chanterelles, reserving the liquid, and distribute among the ramekins. Pour the custard cream mixture overtop. Place the ramekins on a tray and cover with plastic wrap. Place in the fridge and chill for at least 8 hours (overnight is better). Take the chanterelle syrup and reduce over high heat until the sugar starts to caramelize. Add ¼ cup (60 mL) whipping cream and swirl to dissolve the caramel, reducing until the caramel will coat the back of a spoon. Transfer to a container and chill.
5. Place ramekins in warm water to loosen, then flip onto clean plates. The panna cotta should slip easily from the glass. Give a gentle shake to release the vacuum (if needed) or dip back into the warm water to slightly melt the outer edge. Serve with the caramel sauce and fresh fruit or berries.

WILDFLOWER HONEY-GLAZED OYSTER MUSHROOM FRITTERS

MAKES ABOUT 24 PIECES

A range of 350–375°F (180–190°C) is the prime zone for frying. At this temperature, moisture in the batter will evaporate quickly and keep the batter from absorbing too much oil. Use a deep pot with at least 4 inches (10 cm) of headroom on the side since the oil will expand when the fritters are added.

Fritter batter
2 eggs, separated
½ cup (125 mL) milk
1 cup (250 mL) flour
1 tsp (5 mL) baking powder
1 tsp (5 mL) salt

Glaze
1 Tbsp (15 mL) wildflower honey
2 Tbsp (30 mL) butter
4 cups (1 L) grapeseed oil
2 cups (500 mL) oyster mushroom pieces
1 tsp (5 mL) toasted sesame seeds

1. In a mixer, add the egg whites and whisk to a soft peak. Set aside in the fridge while you make the batter. In a bowl, combine the milk and egg yolks, whisking until smooth. In a second bowl, mix the flour, baking powder, and salt. Add to the milk mixture and stir until smooth. Fold in the egg whites.
2. In a saucepan, melt the honey, then remove from the heat and whisk in the butter. Keep warm until needed.
3. Heat the oil to 365°F (185°C), using a thermometer for the best results. Dip the oyster mushrooms in the batter and then gently place in the oil. Repeat until the fat is at a full boil. Gently stir the mixture to distribute the fritters. When golden brown, about 4–5 minutes, remove the fritters using a slotted spoon, drain, and place on a tray lined with paper towels. Repeat with remaining mushrooms and batter.
4. Transfer fritters to serving plates or a platter. Drizzle with the honey sauce and top with toasted sesame seeds.

HONEY-TRUFFLE ICE CREAM

MAKES ABOUT 6 CUPS (1.5 L)

Use black truffle honey if possible; white truffles add a garlic note that is at odds with the sweet ice cream (unless you like garlic ice cream!). I use a small home ice cream maker (the type where you freeze the bowl). Make sure the bowl has been in the freezer for at least 24 hours for the best results. Honey ice creams tend to become rock hard after a day or so. Use up quickly for the best texture.

4 cups (1 L) whipping cream
1 tsp (5 mL) pure vanilla extract
½ cup (125 mL) truffle honey (or honey)
¼ cup (60 mL) white sugar
8 egg yolks

1. In a large saucepan, combine the whipping cream, vanilla, and honey. Bring to a boil. Watch carefully or it will boil over quickly and leave a mess. Just when the mixture begins to boil, remove from the stove.
2. Quickly combine the sugar and egg yolks in a mixing bowl, whisking until smooth. Pour in half of the hot mixture and whisk gently until smooth. With a spatula, scrape the mixture back into the hot cream pan. Whisk constantly over medium heat until the mixture begins to thicken, about 1–2 minutes. Do not allow the mixture to boil. Remove from the heat, strain into a storage container, and let cool to room temperature. Cover tightly and chill.
3. Place the mixture in an ice cream machine and process as directed by the manufacturer's instructions.
4. When smooth and chilled, remove ice cream and place in a plastic container. Freeze until needed. This ice cream is best after about 1 hour in the freezer. If the ice cream is rock hard, let soften at room temperature before serving.

BEVERAGES

PINE MUSHROOM VODKA

MAKES 1 QUART (1 L)

This makes an excellent pine mushroom martini. You can use any dried mushroom, like chanterelle, shiitake, oyster, porcini, or morel, to create a similar infusion; use about 2 ounces (60 g) of dried mushrooms per bottle of vodka. You can also use white rum or sake for variation. Make sure to strain the alcohol before using to remove any grit or silt that may have adhered to the dry mushrooms. For an enhanced forest flavour, you can also add fir, spruce, or pine needles to the infusion for an interesting and delicious effect.

1 cup (250 mL) cleaned and peeled pine mushroom buttons
26 oz (750 mL) good-quality vodka

1. Place the mushrooms in a clean 1 quart (1 L) mason jar. Top up with the vodka and screw on the top. Set on your counter for 1 week. The mixture can be strained, or you can keep the whole batch in the fridge.

TRUFFLE VODKA

MAKES 26 OUNCES (750 ML)

Excellent when served in a truffle martini. Try sipping the iced vodka with caviar or smoked salmon.

---

1 oz (28 g) black or white truffle
26 oz (750 mL) good-quality vodka (or brandy)

---

1. Grate the truffle into a bowl and cover with a little vodka. With a funnel, pour the mixture back into the vodka bottle (or use a mason jar). Make sure to remove all the truffle from the bowl and the funnel. Label the bottle and place in the fridge (the flavour will begin to infuse almost immediately). The vodka is ready for use in a couple of days. Once the vodka is infused, store the bottle in the freezer.

MUSHROOM AND GINGER TEA

MAKES 4 CUPS (1 L)

Try this restorative tea the next time you feel any symptoms of a cold, flu, or sore throat. It even picks you up when you feel tired or weak.

2 dried shiitake mushroom caps
2 fresh ginger slices
4 cups (1 L) boiling water

1. Rinse the shiitake caps under warm water and add to a teapot. Add the ginger slices and cover with the boiling water. Let the tea steep for about 5 minutes. Serve hot. You can refresh the pot with more hot water for a second infusion; let the pot sit for 5–7 minutes before serving.

KOMBUCHA TEA

MAKES ABOUT 3 QUARTS (3 L)

Also known as Manchurian mushroom tea, kombucha is a complex mix of bacteria and yeasts that form a SCOBY (symbiotic culture of bacteria and yeast). It is not technically a mushroom but it is used as a medicinal and health-promoting drink all over the world. The tea must be kept in a sterile environment and is prone to being attacked by harmful bacteria and moulds if not handled properly. Kombucha culture starter kits are available in health food stores, can be ordered off the Internet, or can be obtained from a friend already growing the culture.

1 cup (250 mL) maple syrup
⅓ oz (10 g) green or black tea (3 tea bags)
1 kombucha starter kit

1. Add 3 quarts (3 L) water to a stainless steel saucepan and bring to a boil. Add the maple syrup and tea. Remove from heat and let cool to room temperature. Remove the tea bags (or strain) into a large (3–4 quarts [3–4 L]) glass jar. Add the kombucha culture, cover the mouth with cheesecloth, and secure with a large rubber band. Leave on the counter for about 1 week and up to 2 weeks (the tea will become more acidic as it sits).
2. At this point, you can strain the tea and store in the fridge. Each time you make a batch of tea, the SCOBY will form a raft with the original kombucha, creating a "mother," and underneath, a new culture, or "baby" raft. When you drain the liquid these can be separated like two pancakes. Use the new culture to start the next batch of tea. The old culture can be used 2–3 more times but will eventually become prone to contamination by other bacteria and moulds. It is very important to handle the raft with clean hands and use clean utensils when transferring and storing the tea. The finished tea will last for several months if refrigerated and kept in a sealed container.

REISHI TEA

MAKES 4 CUPS (1 L)

Reishi (*Ganoderma lucidum*) is a polypore that becomes very tough when dried. To extract the most medicinal benefits from the mushroom, you must grind it into a fine powder. You can buy reishi as slices or as a pre-made powder. The slices are fairly easy to grind in a spice (or coffee) grinder.

1 Tbsp (15 mL) ground reishi

1. Bring 4 cups (1 L) water to boil in a stainless steel saucepan. Add the reishi, reduce heat to a simmer and boil for about 2 hours. Cool the tea and drink diluted with fresh water. Can be made in larger batches and stored for several days.

REISHI EXTRACT

MAKES 26 OUNCES (750 ML)

The hot water extraction of reishi is effective as a means to extract many health-promoting properties (mainly through extracting the polysaccharides). Other medicinal properties are best extracted by using alcohol. This method targets a group of compounds known as triterpenes (specifically ganoderic acid). These compounds are thought to target blood purification and may possess anti-carcinogenic properties.

1 cup (250 mL) reishi powder or 2 cups (500 mL) dried reishi slices
26 oz (750 mL) vodka

1. Place the reishi powder or slices in a clean 1 quart (1 L) mason jar. Cover with the vodka and place on the counter for about 4 weeks, shaking occasionally. After about 1 month, the liquid should be the colour of dark tea. Strain the liquid through a coffee filter and place in a clean, dark-coloured jar or bottle. If stored in a cool, dark place, the liquid will last for about 2 years. To use as a tincture, place 1 teaspoon (5 mL) in a glass of cold water and drink daily.

ACKNOWLEDGEMENTS

This book has been a labour of love, in progress for the past twenty years. I would like to thank my family, particularly my wife, Lynn, who has been my patient partner for many years. My parents, Bill and Joan, were supportive all my life, encouraging my urges to explore. I'm particularly grateful to my late father for teaching me how to cook and how to successfully blend professional cooking with a good family life. Lynn's father, Ken Wilkinson, was also very kind to us and was an important part of our life. We miss both of these unique men.

I have had many mycology teachers over the years and have met a number of weird and wonderful characters who have guided me along the way and kept my mushroom experience a happy one. Many foraging friends have helped me source products and together we have spent blissful days in the forests and fields. I would particularly like to thank Eric Whitehead and his family (partner, Michelle, and daughter, Milla), who bring me amazing porcini and morel mushrooms—and are just nice people in general.

TouchWood Editions has been great to work with. It all started with a call from Pat Touchie, who introduced me to publisher Ruth Linka. Her team has been professional from the beginning, with an admirable attention to detail. Holland Gidney and Cailey Cavallin have much improved the text with their editing skills. Pete Kohut did a great job designing the style and layout of the book, and Emily Shorthouse was in charge of publicity and promotion for this fine work. For their work on the revised edition, I would like to thank publisher Tori Elliott, editorial coordinator Kate Kennedy, publicist Curtis Samuel, designer Sara Loos, and indexer Brittany Vesterback. In the Cowichan Valley, I would like to thank Mary Ann Watson (and her great family: Marvin, Joshua, and Eli) for helping me to promote the farm and the book.

I would also like to thank my constant foraging companions—my border collies. Cooper passed away in 2011 after many years of faithful service, and Oliver has jumped in as chief foraging dog and chaser of squirrels. They help make life interesting and fun. Lastly I would like to thank you, the reader—for supporting books and taking the time to discover the world of fungi.

RESOURCES

Websites

Mycological Societies

Alberta Mycological Society *albertamushrooms.ca*
Cercle des Mycologues de Montreal *mycomontreal.qc.ca*
Mycological Society of Toronto *myctor.org*
North American Mycological Association *namyco.org*
South Vancouver Island Mycological Society *svims.ca*
Vancouver Mycological Society *vanmyco.com*

Commercial Associations

Mushroom Council *mushroomcouncil.org*
Mushrooms Canada *mushrooms.ca*
Oregon Truffle Festival *oregontrufflefestival.org*

Mushroom Experts

Larry Evans *fungaljungal.org*
Taylor Lockwood *taylorlockwood.com*
Tom Volk's Fungi *botit.botany.wisc.edu/toms_fungi*

Identification Resources

Foraging Resources *foraging.com*
Mushroom Expert *mushroomexpert.com*
MykoWeb *mykoweb.com*

Mushroom Growing Kits

Back to the Roots Oyster Kits *backtotheroots.com*
Circular Harvest *circularharvest.ca*
Foragers Galley *foragersgalley.com*
Grow Mushrooms Canada *growmushroomscanada.ca*
Paul Stamets's Fungi Perfecti *fungi.com*

Selected Mushroom and Truffle Suppliers

Earthy Delights *earthy.com*
Mikuni Wild Harvest *mikuniwildharvest.com*
Misty Mountain Specialties *mistymt.com*
Pacific Rim Mushrooms *pacrimmushrooms.com*
Ponderosa Mushrooms *ponderosamushrooms.com*
Untamed Feast *untamedfeast.com*
Wine Forest Wild Foods *wineforest.com*

Books

General Interest

Chanterelle Dreams, Amanita Nightmares: The Love, Lore, and Mystique of Mushrooms, Greg Marley, Chelsea Green Publishing, 2010

The Fungal Pharmacy: The Complete Guide to Medicinal Mushrooms and Lichen of North America, Robert Rogers, North Atlantic Books, 2011

Medicinal Mushrooms of North America, Robert Rogers and Duane J. Sept, Calypso Publishing, 2020

Mushroom, Nicholas P. Money, Oxford University Press USA, 2011

Mycophilia: Revelations from the Weird World of Mushrooms, Eugenia Bone, Rodale Books, 2011

Stalking the Wild Asparagus, Euell Gibbons, Alan C. Hood & Company, 1962

Identification

100 Edible Mushrooms, Michael Kuo, University of Michigan Press, 2007

All That the Rain Promises and More: A Hip Pocket Guide to Western Mushrooms, David Arora, Ten Speed Press, 1991

The Book of Fungi: A Life-Size Guide to Six Hundred Species from Around the World, Peter Roberts and Shelly Evans, University of Chicago Press, 2011

Common Mushrooms of the Northwest: Alaska, Western Canada and the Northwestern United States, J. Duane Sept, Calypso Publishing, 2006

The Complete Mushroom Hunter: An Illustrated Guide to Finding, Harvesting, and Enjoying Wild Mushrooms, Gary Lincoff, Quarry Books, 2010

A Field Guide to Mushrooms: North America (Peterson Field Guides), Kent McKnight and Vera McKnight, Houghton Mifflin, 1998

Fruits of the Forest: A field guide to Pacific Northwest Edible Mushrooms, Daniel Winkler, Skipstone Books, 2023

Mushroom Picker's Foolproof Field Guide: The Expert Guide to Identifying, Picking and Using Wild Mushrooms, Peter Jordan, Anness, 2010

Mushrooms and Other Fungi of North America, Roger Phillips, Firefly Books, 2010
Mushrooms Demystified, David Arora, Ten Speed Press, 1986
Mushrooms of British Columbia, Andy MacKinnon and Kem Luther, Royal BC Museum, 2021
Mushrooms of the Pacific Northwest, Steve Trudel and Joe Ammirati, Timber Press Field Guide, 2009
National Audubon Society Field Guide to North American Mushrooms (National Audubon Society Field Guides), Gary Lincoff, Knopf, 1981
North American Boletes: A Color Guide to the Fleshy Pored Mushrooms, Alan Bessette, William Roody, and Arleen Bessette, Syracuse University Press, 2010

Cultivation

Growing Gourmet and Medicinal Mushrooms, Paul Stamets, Ten Speed Press, 2000
Medicinal Mushrooms: An Exploration of Tradition, Healing, & Culture, Christopher Hobbs and Harriet Beinfield, Botanica Press, 2003
Mycelium Running: How Mushrooms Can Help Save the World, Paul Stamets, Ten Speed Press, 2005

Cookbooks

The Complete Mushroom Book: The Quiet Hunt, Antonio Carlucci, Quadrille Publishing Ltd., 2005
Pacific Feast: A Cook's Guide to West Coast Foraging and Cuisine, Jennifer Hahn, Skipstone, 2010
The Paley's Place Cookbook: Recipes and Stories from the Pacific Northwest, Vitaly Paley and Kimberly Paley, Ten Speed Press, 2008
The Savoury Mushroom: Cooking with Wild and Cultivated Mushrooms, Bill Jones, Raincoast Books, 2000
Wild Mushrooms (Northwest Homegrown Cookbook Series), Cynthia Nims, Westwinds Press, 2004
The Wild Table: Seasonal Foraged Food and Recipes, Connie Green and Sarah Scott, Viking Studio, 2010

INDEX

C

D

E

F

G

H

I

R

S

T

U

V

W

Y

Z